Conquer Year 5 Maths with CGP!

Ready to test the key facts and methods in Year 5 Maths? Once pupils have got to grips with all the content in our matching Year 5 Maths Knowledge Organiser, they can check how much they've learned with our Knowledge Retriever!

With bonus mixed practice quizzes and a full set of answers too, this book has everything Year 5 pupils need for Maths success!

CGP – still the best! ☺

Our sole aim here at CGP is to produce the highest quality books — carefully written, immaculately presented and dangerously close to being funny.

Then we work our socks off to get them out to you — at the cheapest possible prices.

Contents

How to Use This Book 1

Number and Place Value
Number Basics 2
Powers of 10 and Rounding 4
Number Facts 6
Prime Numbers 8
Number and Place Value Quiz 10

Calculations
Adding and Subtracting 12
Multiplying and Dividing 14
Calculations Quiz 16

Fractions, Decimals & Percentages
Fractions 18
Fraction Calculations 20
Decimals 22
Fractions, Decimals & Percentages 24
Fractions, Decimals & Percentages Quiz 26

Measurement
Converting Units 28
Perimeter, Area and Volume 30
Measurement Quiz 32

Geometry
Angles 34
Shapes 36
Coordinates & Transformations 38
Geometry Quiz 40

Statistics
Line Graphs 42
Tables 44
Statistics Quiz 46

End of Year Quiz 48

Answers 54

Published by CGP

Editors: Sarah George, Rachel Hickman, Hannah Lawson, Sean McParland, Ali Palin, Sarah Pattison and Dave Ryan.

With thanks to Ruth Greenhalgh and Alison Griffin for the proofreading.

With thanks to Jan Greenway for the copyright research.

ISBN: 978 1 78908 873 1

Printed by Elanders Ltd, Newcastle upon Tyne.
Clipart from Corel®

Based on the classic CGP style created by Richard Parsons.

Text, design, layout and original illustrations
© Coordination Group Publications Ltd. (CGP) 2022
All rights reserved.

Photocopying this book is not permitted, even if you have a CLA licence.
Extra copies are available from CGP with next day delivery. • 0800 1712 712 • www.cgpbooks.co.uk

How to Use This Book

Every page in this book has a matching page in the Year 5 Maths **Knowledge Organiser**. Before filling in the pages in this book, you should have learnt about the topic in your lessons at school and the Knowledge Organiser.

Read the page and fill in the dotted lines. You might need to write one word, several words, a number or a symbol. Sometimes the first letter of a word is given to help you.

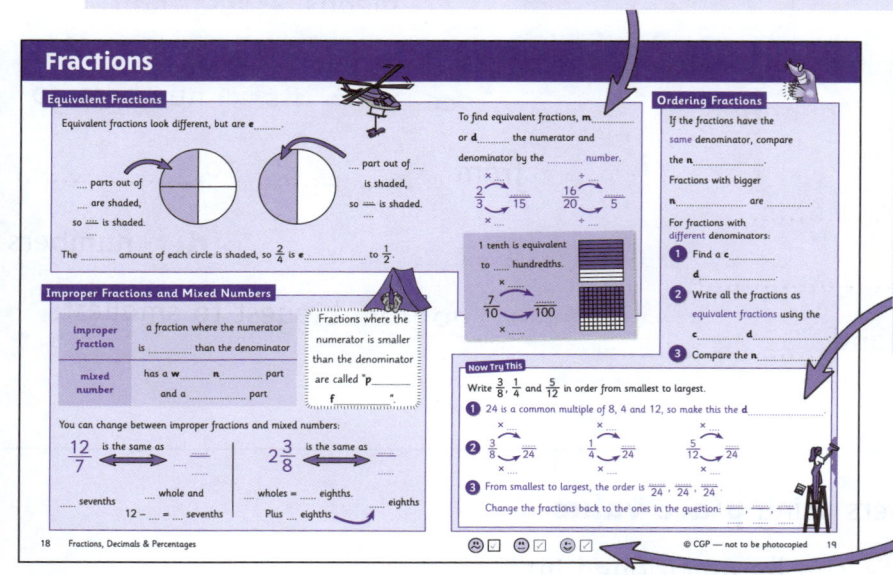

'Now Try This' boxes are a chance to have a go at the topic. You may need to draw or complete diagrams, as well as fill in dotted lines.

Tick the smiley face that shows how happy you feel with the page.

Once you've finished a page, use the answers at the back of the book to check your work. You might have used a different word to fill in the gap — that's okay, as long as the word has the same meaning.

There are also quizzes throughout the book:
- There is a quiz at the end of each section. These quizzes test a mix of content from the previous few pages. There is also a bigger quiz at the end, which covers everything from the book.
- Answers to the quizzes are at the back of the book. Write your score in the box at the end of each quiz.

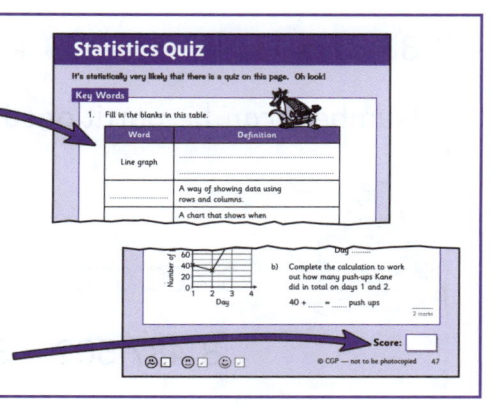

Number Basics

Place Value

millions → 9 254 318

ten thousands
hundreds

This number is:

nine million, ...

and ....,

.... and ....

Comparing and Ordering

To compare two or more numbers, look at the digits in each place value column.

.... means "is greater than".

.... means "is less than".

Ascending order: numbers go from .... to ....

D.................. **order**: numbers go from biggest to smallest.

Partitioning

You can partition numbers using **place value**.

The number **3 487 502** can be partitioned into 3 millions,

.... hundred thousands, ... ten thousands, ... thousands, ... hundreds and .... ones.

M	HTh	TTh	Th	H	T	O
....	....	....	....	....	0	....

There aren't any **t**.......... .

3 487 502 = 3 000 000 + ...00 000 + 80 000 + ...000 + ...00 + ...

Numbers can be partitioned in other ways too:

3 487 502
├─ 3 400 000
├─ 85 000
├─ ....
└─ 2

3 487 502 = 3 400 000 + 85 000 + ... + 2

2   Number and Place Value

Now Try This
Use < or > to make the statement below correct.

325 604 __ 305 624

Both numbers have
.... hundred thousands.

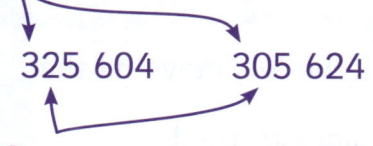

325 604   305 624

2 is .... than 0.

So 325 604 .... 305 624

Now Try This
Put these numbers into ascending order:
132, 1051, 211, 141

1051 is the only number with a
t.................. digit, so it's the b................
.... has 2 hundreds, 132 and 141 have ... hundred. 2 is .... than 1, so 211 is next ....
141 has .... tens, 132 has .... tens.
4 is .... than 3, so .... is bigger.
So the order is ...., ..., ..., ...

Negative Numbers
Negative numbers are numbers l.......... t.......... zero.

Use n.............. l.......... to calculate with them.

To find the difference between two numbers, count the p.............. between them.

Now Try This
Find the difference between 5 and -3.

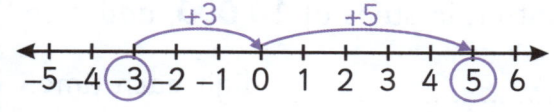

$+3$ $+5$
$-5\ -4\ (-3)\ -2\ -1\ 0\ 1\ 2\ 3\ 4\ (5)\ 6$

Between -3 and 0 there are .... places.

Between 0 and 5 there are .... places.

So the difference is .... + ... = ...

To add, find your starting point and count .... To subtract, find your starting point and count ....

Now Try This
What is $-1 - 12$?

1. Start at ..... .
2. Count .... 10 places.
3. Then count back .... places.

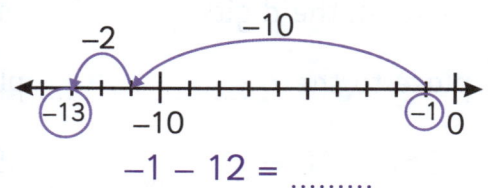

-2 -10
$(-13)\quad -10 \quad\quad\quad (-1)\ 0$

$-1 - 12 =$ ....

Powers of 10 and Rounding

Counting in Powers of 10

Power of 10: a ... followed by zeros. E.g. 10, 100, ..., ..., etc.

To count on in steps of a power of 10, add .... to the digit matching the power.

To count on from **25 384** in steps of **100**, add 1 to the **h**................ digit each time.

25 384 → 25 _ 84 → 25 _ 84
         +1   +1

To count on in steps of **10 000**, add 1 to the **t**........................ digit each time.

To count back in steps of a power of 10, subtract .... from the digit matching the power.

Now Try This

Count back from 18 324 in steps of 1000. Stop after 3 steps.

1<u>8</u> 324   1_ 324   1_ 324   1_ 324
       −1   −1   −1

Multiplying by 10, 100, 1000

To multiply by **10**, move all the digits .... place to the **l**............

51 × 10 = ...

To multiply by **100**, move all the digits .... places to the **l**............

51 × 100 = ...

To multiply by **1000**, move all the digits .... places to the **l**............

51 × 1000 = ...

Dividing by 10, 100, 1000

To divide by **10**, move all the digits .... place to the **r**............

350 ÷ 10 = ...

To divide by **100**, move all the digits .... places to the **r**............

350 ÷ 100 = ...

To divide by **1000**, move all the digits .... places to the **r**............

350 ÷ 1000 = ...

Number and Place Value

Rounding Whole Numbers

You can round whole numbers to the nearest 10, 100, 1000, etc.

1 Find the two possible answers.

2 Look at the digit to the r.......... of the place being rounded to — the decider.

3 If the decider is less than ...., then round .... If the decider is ...., then round up.

Now Try This

Round 2067 to the nearest ten.

2067 is between 20....0 and 20....0.

The decider is .... ⟶ 2067

.... is more than 5, so round 2067 .... to ....

Move all the digits .... places to the ....

Fill spaces before the decimal point with ....

$32.8 \times 1000 =$ ....

TTh	Th	H	T	O	t^{th}
			3	2 .	8
3	....	....	....	.... .	

Don't add a zero here.

The number of .... tells you how many .... to move the digits.

Fill space before the decimal point with a ....

$6.3 \div 100 =$ ....

O	t^{th}	h^{th}	th^{th}
6 .	3		
.... .	....	....	3

Move all the digits .... places to the ....

Fill the space between the decimal point and the first digit with ....

Number Facts

Multiples

Multiples of a number: the numbers in its times table. E.g. the multiples of 7 are 7, ..., ..., ..., etc.

Rules for spotting multiples:

Multiples of 2	End in **e**.......... numbers or ....
Multiples of 5	End in .... or ....
Multiples of 10	End in ....

Common multiple of two numbers: a number that is a .... of .... numbers.

Now Try This

Find a common multiple of 8 and 12.

First few multiples of 8:

8   32

First few multiples of 12:

....   36   ......

...... is a common multiple of 8 and 12.

Factors

Factors of a number: **w**.......... **n**.................. that .... exactly into it.

Factors come in **p**.......... that **m**............... together to give the number.

If there's an **o**....... number of factors, the middle factor multiplies by itself.

Square and Cube Numbers

Square number: the number you get when you multiply a number by ....

$4 \times 4 = 4$ squared $= 4^2 = $ ......

$6 \times 6 = $ .... squared $= $ .... $= $ ......

$9 \times 9 = $ .... squared $= $ .... $= $ ......

Square numbers are the **a**.......... in this pattern of squares.

$1 \times 1 = $ ....

$2 \times 2 = $ ....

$3 \times 3 = $ ....

The first few square numbers are 1, 4, 9, 16 and 25.

Now Try This

Find all the factor pairs of 12.

12   1 × .... × 6   3 × ......

The factor pairs are 1 and ......,
...... and 6, and 3 and ....

Common factor of two numbers: a number that is a f............... of b......... numbers.

Now Try This

What are the common factors of 15 and 27?

Factors of 15:   15

Factors of 27:   1   9   ......

.... and .... are the c...............
f............... of 15 and 27.

Roman Numerals

Roman numerals are letters that represent ....

I = 1	V = ...	X = ...	L = 50
C = ...	D = ...		M = 1000

1 **A**...... together numerals that are the *same*. → III = ...

2 Smaller numeral *before* a .... one — subtract. → IX = ...

3 Smaller numeral .... a bigger one — **a**......... . → MC = ...

4 Convert numbers in *stages*:

LXXIX

50 + 10 + ... = ...   10 ... 1 = ...

.... + ... = ...

Cube number: the number you get when you multiply a number by itself ....

2 × 2 × 2 = 2 cubed = 2^3 = ...

4 × 4 × 4 = ... cubed = ... = ...

5 × 5 × 5 = ... cubed = ... = ...

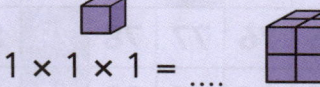

1 × 1 × 1 = ...

2 × 2 × 2 = ...

3 × 3 × 3 = ...

Cube numbers are the **v**............... in this pattern of cubes.

The first few cube numbers are 1, 8, 27 and 64.

Prime Numbers

Prime Numbers

Prime number: has exactly two f............. — .... and ....

A number with more than two f.................. is called a composite number.

1. .... is not a prime number — it only has 1 factor.
2. All prime numbers end in 1, 3, ... or ...., except for .... and .....
3. .... is the only even prime number.

The prime numbers below 20 are: 2, ..., 5, ..., ..., 13, 17 and ....

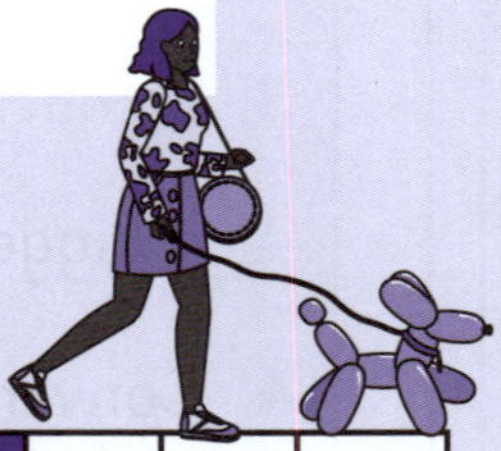

Prime Factors

Whole numbers that aren't prime (apart from 1) are made up of prime numbers multiplied together.

These numbers are called **prime factors**.

To find prime factors:

1. Write down any f............. p........ of the number.
2. Split composite numbers into f............. p............
3. Repeat until all the factors are ....

The shaded squares show the prime numbers up to 100.

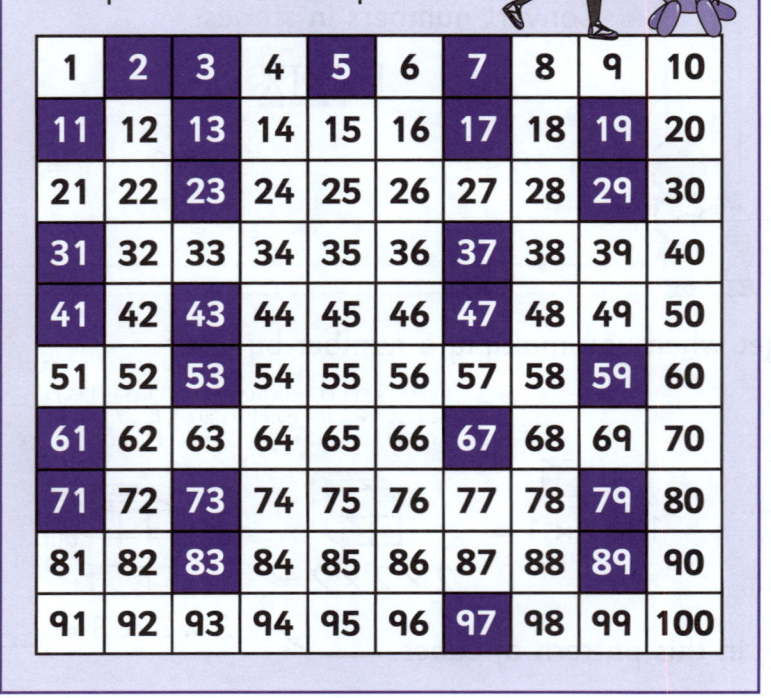

1	2	3	4	5	6	7	8	9	10
11	12	13	14	15	16	17	18	19	20
21	22	23	24	25	26	27	28	29	30
31	32	33	34	35	36	37	38	39	40
41	42	43	44	45	46	47	48	49	50
51	52	53	54	55	56	57	58	59	60
61	62	63	64	65	66	67	68	69	70
71	72	73	74	75	76	77	78	79	80
81	82	83	84	85	86	87	88	89	90
91	92	93	94	95	96	97	98	99	100

Number and Place Value

Checking if a Number is Prime

1 Does the number end in 1, 3, ... or ....?
— Yes → **2** Does it have exactly two f................?
  — Yes → **3** Prime
  — No → Not prime
— No → Is the number .... or ....?
  — Yes → Prime
  — No → Not prime

EXAMPLE
Which prime numbers multiply together to make 63?

7 is a .... number.

Split .... into a factor pair.

63
/ \
7 ....
   / \
  ....

$63 = 7 \times .... \times ....$, so the prime numbers are ...., ... and 7.

Now Try This
Which of the following numbers are prime numbers?

27   53   49   62   75   31

27, 53, 49, and 31 end in a 1, 3, 7 or 9, so could be ....

Factors of 27: ....

Factors of 53: ....

Factors of 49: ....

Factors of 31: ....

So .... and .... are prime numbers.

EXAMPLE
Find the prime factors of 24.

24
/ \
2 ....
   / \
  4 ....
  / \
 ....

2 is a .... number. Split ...... into a factor pair.

.... is a prime number. Split 4 into a factor pair.

All of the factors are prime numbers, so the prime factors of 24 are .... and .... .

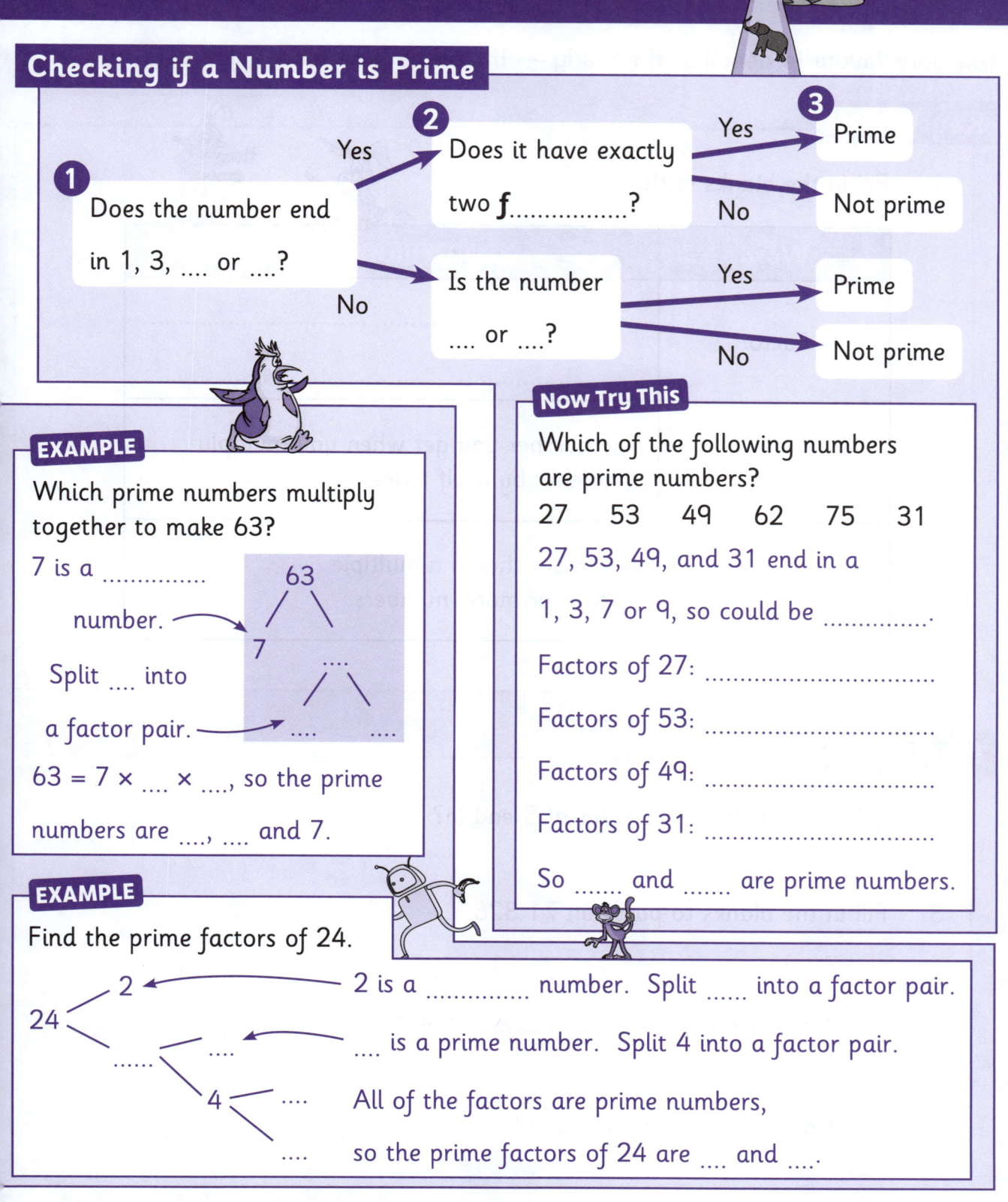

Number and Place Value Quiz

Get your favourite pencil at the ready — it's prime time for a quick quiz.

Key Words

1. Fill in the blanks in this table.

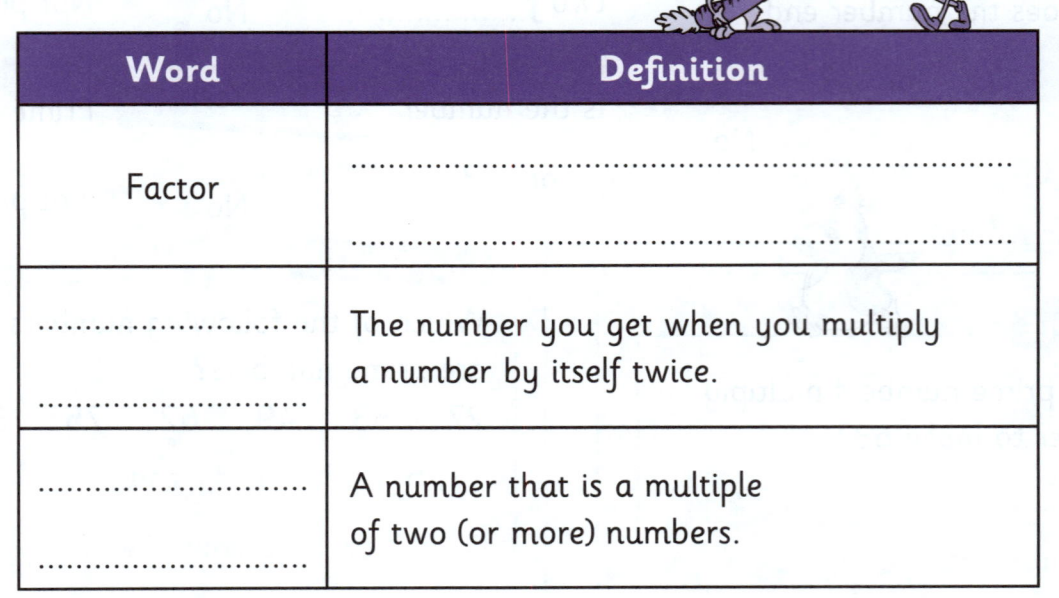

Word	Definition
Factor	....
....	The number you get when you multiply a number by itself twice.
....	A number that is a multiple of two (or more) numbers.

3 marks

Now Try These

2. What digits do all multiples of 5 end in? .... or ....

   2 marks

3. Fill in the blanks to partition 71 326.

    7 ...., 1 ....,

    3 hundreds, 2 .... and 6 ....

   4 marks

4. What does the symbol '<' mean?   ....

   1 mark

10 Number and Place Value

5. Circle the number in the list below that is a square number.

    20   5   42   36   8

    1 mark

6. How do you count back in powers of 10?

    ....

    1 mark

7. 8516 is being rounded to the nearest thousand.

    a) Which digit is the decider? ....

    b) Should it be rounded up or down? ....

    2 marks

8. How should you move the digits when multiplying by 1000?

    ....

    1 mark

9. Lola says that 21 is a prime number because it ends in a 1. Explain why she is wrong.

    ....

    1 mark

10. What is the value of the Roman numeral M? ....

    1 mark

11. Jeremy is finding the prime factors of 30. He starts by writing down 30 = 5 × 6. What should he do next?

    ....

    1 mark

Score:

Adding and Subtracting

Adding in Columns

Now Try This

Work out 62 832 + 13 795.

1 Add the o.......... column.

```
 TTh Th  H  T  O
  6  2  8  3  2
+ 1  3  7  9  5
_____
              ....
```

2 Add the t.......... column.

```
 TTh Th  H  T  O
  6  2  8  3  2
+ 1  3  7  9  5
_____
           ....
```

3 + ... = ..., so put .... in the .... column and carry .... to the .... column.

3 Add the h.................. column.

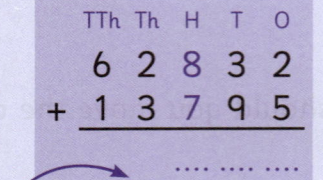

```
 TTh Th  H  T  O
  6  2  8  3  2
+ 1  3  7  9  5
_____
        .... .... ....
```

Remember to add any carried digits.

8 + ... + ... = ..., so put .... in the .... column and carry .... to the .... column.

4 Subtract the t..........: .... − .... = ...
Then the h..................:
.... − .... = ...

```
 H  T  O . t
 8  3  5 . 3
−5  1  6 . 2
_____
 .... .... . ....
```

So 835.3 − 516.2 = ...

Subtracting in Columns

Now Try This

Find 835.3 − 516.2

1 Line up the decimal points.

```
 H  T  O . t
 8  3  5 . 3
−5  1  6 . 2
_____
         . ....
```

2 Subtract the t..............:

.... − .... = ...

3 Subtract the o.......... You can't do .... − 6, so exchange 1 ten for 10 ones. Then ...... − 6 = ...

```
 H  T  O . t
 8  3  5 . 3
−5  1  6 . 2
_____
     .... . ....
```

12   Calculations

Addition and Subtraction Problems

Read the question and pick out the key information.

Then turn it into number sentences.

Now Try This

Max has £7.50. He is given £5.95, then he spends £10.40. How much money does he have now?

Max had £.......... + £.......... = £..........

Now Max has £.......... − £.......... = £..........

④ Add the thousands column and then the ten thousands column.

```
  TTh Th  H  T  O
   6  2   8  3  2
+  1  3   7  9  5
  ................
     ........
```

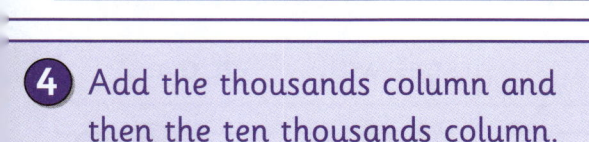

So 62 832 + 13 795 = ...

Mental Calculations

Now Try This

Use partitioning to find 5024 + 3090.

5024 + 3090

.... + 3000 + 20 + ... + ...

.... + ... + ... = ...

For decimal sums, do a whole-number calculation and then adjust the answer.

Now Try This

What is 9.3 − 4.8?

Multiply both numbers by ......

to get whole numbers:

93 − ...... = ...

Adjust by dividing by ......:

9.3 − 4.8 = ... ÷ ...... = ...

Checking Answers

You can use rounding to

e.................. answers.

Now Try This

Li works out that 38.9 − 17.3 = 31.6. Use estimation to check Li's answer.

To the nearest whole number, 38.9 rounds to ...... and 17.3 rounds to ......

...... − ...... = ...

This is not close to ...., so Li is wrong.

Multiplying and Dividing

Long Multiplication

P............... the 2-digit number.

M............... by each part

separately. Then a....... together.

Now Try This

Calculate 2317 × 23.

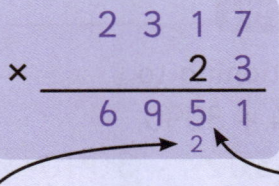

1 Find 2317 × ....

```
    2 3 1 7
  ×     2 3
    6 9 5 1
          2
```

3 × 7 = ..., so put

the .... in the .... column

and carry .... to the .... column.

3 × 10 = ..., plus the carried ...... is ....

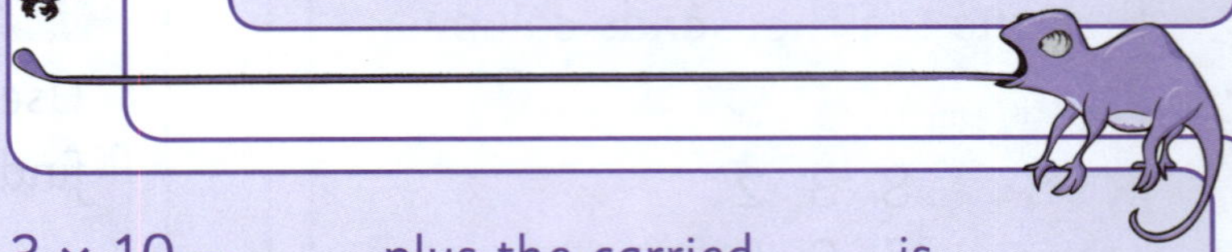

2 Find 2317 × ......

```
    2 3 1 7
  ×     2 3
    6 9 5 1
    4 6 3 4 0
            1
```

20 × 10 = ...,

plus the carried

.... is ....

20 × 7 = ..., so put .... and 0

in the correct columns and carry

.... to the .... column.

Written Division

Now Try This

What is 4682 divided by 5?

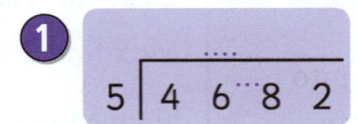

1
```
        ....
   5 ) 4 6 ·· 8 2
```

5 × 9 = ..., so 5 goes into 46

.... times with .... left over.

3 A....... the answers together.

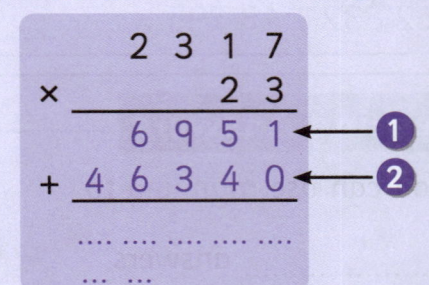

```
    2 3 1 7
  ×     2 3
    6 9 5 1  ← 1
  + 4 6 3 4 0  ← 2
    .... .... .... .... ....
    ... ...
```

2317 × 23 = 6951 + 46 340

= ....

Wordy Problems

Pick out the key information
and write the problem as
a number sentence.

2) 5) 4 6 8 2

5 × 3 = ..., so 5 goes into 18 .... times with .... left over.

3) 5) 4 6 8 2 r ....

5 × 6 = ..., so 5 goes into 32 .... times with .... left over.

So 4682 ÷ 5 = ... remainder ....

The remainder can be written as a **f**................... ....

or as a **d**................. ....

Mental Calculations

To multiply in your head, change the calculation to something easier to deal with.

Now Try This

Tony swims 28 lengths every day. How many lengths does he swim in 6 days?

Tony swims ...... × .... lengths in total.

28 = 30 − ...., so work out

30 × 6 and .... × 6, then subtract:

30 × 6 = ... and .... × 6 = ...

He swims .... − ...... = ... lengths.

You can use partitioning to divide.

Now Try This

Use partitioning to find 114 ÷ 6.

114 = 60 + ...

So work out 60 ÷ 6 and .... ÷ 6, then add the answers together:

60 ÷ 6 = ... and .... ÷ 6 = ...

So 114 ÷ 6 = ... + ... = ...

Now Try This

Rhea spent £8. Anil spent three times as much money as Rhea. Cleo spent one quarter of what Anil spent. How much money did Cleo spend?

Anil spent £8 × .... = £....... So Cleo spent £....... ÷ .... = £....

Calculations Quiz

You + this wonderful quiz = a recipe for maths success...

Key Words

1. Fill in the blanks in this table.

Word	Definition
....	The amount that is left over after a division.
....	A way to check answers, e.g. by rounding.

   2 marks

Now Try These

2. A remainder can be given as a number.
   Give two other ways that you could give a remainder.

   1. ....   2. ....

   2 marks

3. Sophie works out 41.8 + 29.6 = 64.2. By rounding to the nearest whole number, check whether her answer is right or wrong.

   ....

   ....

   1 mark

4. How could you use the calculation 53 + 17 to work out 5.3 + 1.7?

   ....

   ....

   1 mark

5. Omar wants to work out 3892 − 1736 by subtracting in columns, but he can't do 2 − 6. What should he do instead?

   ....

   ....

   1 mark

6. Randall is working out 4372 × 18 using long multiplication.

   a) What should he partition 18 into?   .... and ....

   b) What is the last thing he needs to do, after multiplying by each part separately?

      ....

   2 marks

7. Petra is working out 38 723 + 12 546 by adding in columns.

   a) Which place value column should she add first?

      ....

   b) When she adds the digits in the hundreds column, she gets 7 + 5 = 12. She writes the 2 in the hundreds column. What should she do next?

      ....

   2 marks

8. Mary works out 2716 ÷ 4 using written division. She writes out the calculation as shown on the right.

   4) 2 7 [B] 1 6   [A above]

   a) What number goes in box A?   ....

   b) What number goes in box B?   ....

   2 marks

Score:

Fractions

Equivalent Fractions

Equivalent fractions look different, but are **e**..........

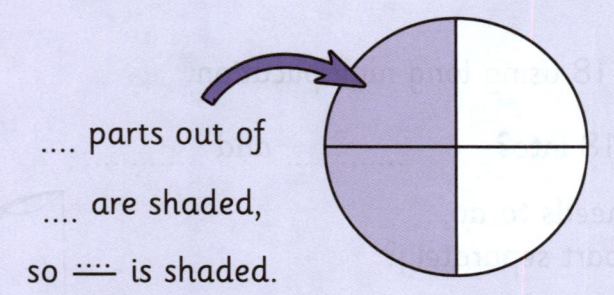

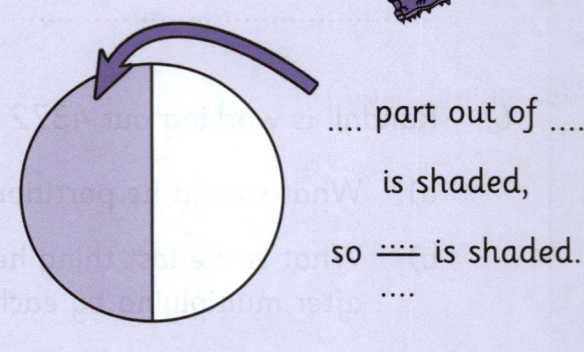

.... parts out of .... are shaded, so $\frac{....}{....}$ is shaded.

.... part out of .... is shaded, so $\frac{....}{....}$ is shaded.

The .... amount of each circle is shaded, so $\frac{2}{4}$ is **e**...................... to $\frac{1}{2}$.

Improper Fractions and Mixed Numbers

improper fraction	a fraction where the numerator is .... than the denominator
mixed number	has a **w**............ **n**................ part and a .... part

Fractions where the numerator is smaller than the denominator are called "**p**...................... **f**......................".

You can change between improper fractions and mixed numbers:

$\frac{12}{7}$ is the same as $\frac{....}{....}$

...... sevenths

.... whole and

$12 - .... = ...$ sevenths

$2\frac{3}{8}$ is the same as $\frac{....}{....}$

.... wholes = ... eighths.

Plus .... eighths

...... eighths

18   Fractions, Decimals & Percentages

To find equivalent fractions, **m**................ or **d**............ the numerator and denominator by the .... number.

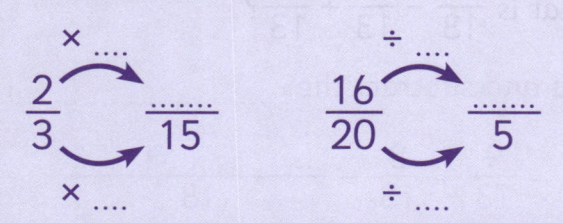

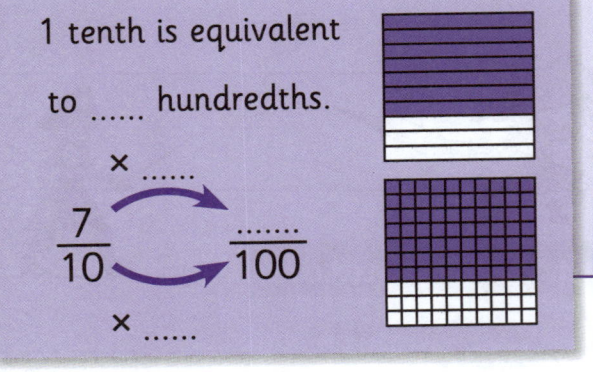

$\frac{2}{3} \rightarrow \frac{......}{15}$ $\frac{16}{20} \rightarrow \frac{......}{5}$

1 tenth is equivalent to ...... hundredths.

$\frac{7}{10} \rightarrow \frac{......}{100}$

Ordering Fractions

If the fractions have the same denominator, compare the **n**........................ Fractions with bigger **n**........................ are ....

For fractions with different denominators:

1. Find a **c**................ **d**........................ .
2. Write all the fractions as equivalent fractions using the **c**................ or **d**........................ .
3. Compare the **n**........................ .

Now Try This

Write $\frac{3}{8}$, $\frac{1}{4}$ and $\frac{5}{12}$ in order from smallest to largest.

1. 24 is a common multiple of 8, 4 and 12, so make this the **d**........................ .

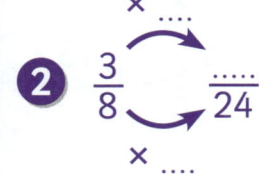

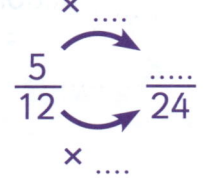

2. $\frac{3}{8} \rightarrow \frac{......}{24}$ $\frac{1}{4} \rightarrow \frac{......}{24}$ $\frac{5}{12} \rightarrow \frac{......}{24}$

3. From smallest to largest, the order is $\frac{......}{24}$, $\frac{......}{24}$, $\frac{......}{24}$.

   Change the fractions back to the ones in the question: $\frac{......}{......}$, $\frac{......}{......}$, $\frac{......}{......}$

Fraction Calculations

Adding and Subtracting — Same Denominator

When fractions have the same denominator, add or subtract the ....

Now Try This

What is $\frac{5}{11} + \frac{8}{11}$?

Add the .... :

$$\frac{5}{11} + \frac{8}{11} = \frac{..... + ...}{11} = \frac{.....}{11}$$

You can also write this as $....\frac{.....}{.....}$.

Now Try This

What is $\frac{18}{13} - \frac{9}{13} + \frac{3}{13}$?

Add and subtract the .... :

$$\frac{18}{13} - \frac{9}{13} + \frac{3}{13} = \frac{..... - ..... + ...}{13}$$

$$= \frac{.....}{13}$$

Adding and Subtracting — Different Denominators

You can only add or subtract fractions if they have the .... denominator.

If the denominators are *different*:

Find .... fractions that have a **c**..................... **d**......................

⬇

Add or subtract the **n**......................

Now Try This

What is $\frac{5}{6} + \frac{4}{9}$?

18 is a common multiple of 6 and 9, so make 18 the **d**......................

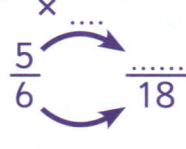

$$\frac{5}{6} \xrightarrow{\times\ ....} \frac{.....}{18} \qquad \frac{4}{9} \xrightarrow{\times\ ....} \frac{.....}{18}$$

$$\frac{5}{6} + \frac{4}{9} = \frac{.....}{18} + \frac{.....}{18}$$

$$= \frac{.............}{18} = \frac{.....}{18}$$

Fractions, Decimals & Percentages

Multiplying Fractions

To multiply a whole number by a fraction, divide by the .... and multiply by the ....

Or you can multiply first, then divide, if that's easier.

When you're dealing with fractions, "of" means " .... ".

Now Try This

What is $\frac{2}{9}$ of 36?

Divide by the ....:

36 ÷ ..... = ...

Multiply by the ....:

..... × ..... = ...

So $\frac{2}{9}$ of 36 = ...

Change mixed numbers to

i........................ f........................

before adding or subtracting them.

Now Try This

What is $1\frac{3}{10} - \frac{8}{15}$?

$1\frac{3}{10} = \frac{.....}{10} + \frac{3}{10} = \frac{.....}{10}$

.... is a common multiple of 10 and 15, so use .... as the common denominator.

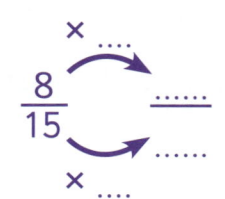

$\frac{.....}{10}$ $\frac{.....}{.....}$ $\frac{8}{15}$ $\frac{.....}{.....}$

$1\frac{3}{10} - \frac{8}{15} = \frac{.....}{.....} - \frac{.....}{.....} = \frac{.....}{.....}$

Partition mixed numbers into whole numbers and fractions, then multiply each part separately.

Now Try This

Work out $2\frac{3}{4} \times 8$.

$2\frac{3}{4} = 2 + \frac{.....}{.....}$

Work out 2 × 8: 2 × 8 = ...

$\frac{1}{4} \times 8 = 8 \div .... = ...,$

so $\frac{3}{4} \times 8 = ... \times .... = ...$.

So $2\frac{3}{4} \times 8 = ... + ... = ...$

You could also change mixed numbers into improper fractions instead, if that's easier.

Decimals

Tenths, Hundredths and Thousandths

Decimals are a way to write a number that isn't a w............ n................
The first few places after the decimal point are the t............,
h........................... and thousandths.

4 . 5 3 7 ← 7 thousandths

4 .... 5 .... 3 ....

0.1 = one .... = $\frac{1}{10}$

.... = one hundredth = $\frac{1}{100}$

0.001 = one thousandth = $\frac{\text{............}}{\text{............}}$

1 tenth = ... thousandths

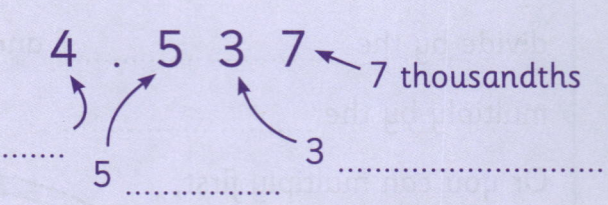

1 .... = 10 thousandths

Now Try This

Write 0.103 as a fraction.

This has .... thousandths.

So the fraction is $\frac{\text{............}}{\text{............}}$.

Rounding Decimals

Each number after the decimal point is called a d............ p......... (d.p.).

0.819
1st d.p. → ↑ ↖ 2nd d.p.
         3rd d.p.

To round decimals:
1. Count the number of d................ p............ you need to keep.
2. Look at the next digit to the .... — the decider.
3. If the decider is less than ......, round .... If the decider is ...., round ....

Now Try This

Round 4.57 to 1 decimal place.

4.5|7

You need to keep 1 decimal place, so the decider is the h........................ digit.

.... is bigger than 5, so round 4.57 .... to ....

22   Fractions, Decimals & Percentages

Writing Decimals as Fractions

To write a decimal as a fraction, look at the tenths, hundredths or thousandths.

$0.7 = 7$ t.............. $= \dfrac{7}{\ldots}$

$0.19 = 19$ h.................... $= \dfrac{19}{\ldots}$

Now Try This

Write 2.081 as a fraction.

This has ..... ones and

...... thousandths.

You can write this as

a mixed number: ..... $\dfrac{\ldots}{\ldots}$

Ordering Decimals

To put decimals in order, look at the digits in each

P.......... v.......... column.

If the digits in one column are the ...., compare the digits in the next column.

Now Try This

Put these decimals in order from smallest to largest: 0.579, 1.34, 0.6, 0.572

Write the numbers in place value columns, keeping the decimal points in line.

0.579	0.579	0.579	....:..........
....:..........	....:..........	....:..........	....:..........
....:..........	0.572	....:..........	0.600
0.572	....:..........	1.340	1.340
Fill in extra zeros so they're the same length.	First order the whole numbers.	Then order the tenths.	0.579 and 0.572 have the same hundredths, so look at the thousandths.

From smallest to largest: ...., ..., ..., ...

Fractions, Decimals & Percentages

Percentage Basics

"Per cent" means "out of ………".

% is a short way of writing per cent, so 40% means "…… out of ………".

………% is the total amount.

Now Try This

23% of pupils in a primary school have blue eyes.
What percentage of pupils at the school don't have blue eyes?

The total is ………%. So ………% − ………% = ………% don't have blue eyes.

Common Conversions

You can write percentages as **d**……………… or **f**………………

Here are some common conversions you should know.

Percentages and Fractions

To convert a percentage to a fraction:

1 Put the percentage as the **n**………………

$$67\% = \frac{\ldots}{\ldots}$$

2 Put ……… as the denominator.

You can also convert fractions to percentages:

$$\frac{23}{50} \overset{\times \ldots}{\underset{\times \ldots}{=}} \frac{\ldots}{100} = \ldots\%$$

Make an **e**……………… **f**………………
with 100 as the denominator.

The ……………… is the percentage.

Percentages and Decimals

To convert a percentage to a decimal, …………… by 100.

$$37\% = 37 \ldots 100 = \ldots$$

Now Try This

$\frac{6}{20}$ of the dogs in a kennel are white, 45% are black and the rest are brown. What percentage of the dogs are brown?

$$\frac{6}{20} \overset{\times \ldots}{\underset{\times \ldots}{=}} \frac{\ldots}{100} = \ldots\% \text{ are white.}$$

……% + 45% = ……% are white or black.

So ……% − ……% = ……% are brown.

$\frac{1}{4}$ $\frac{\ldots}{\ldots}$ $\frac{3}{4}$

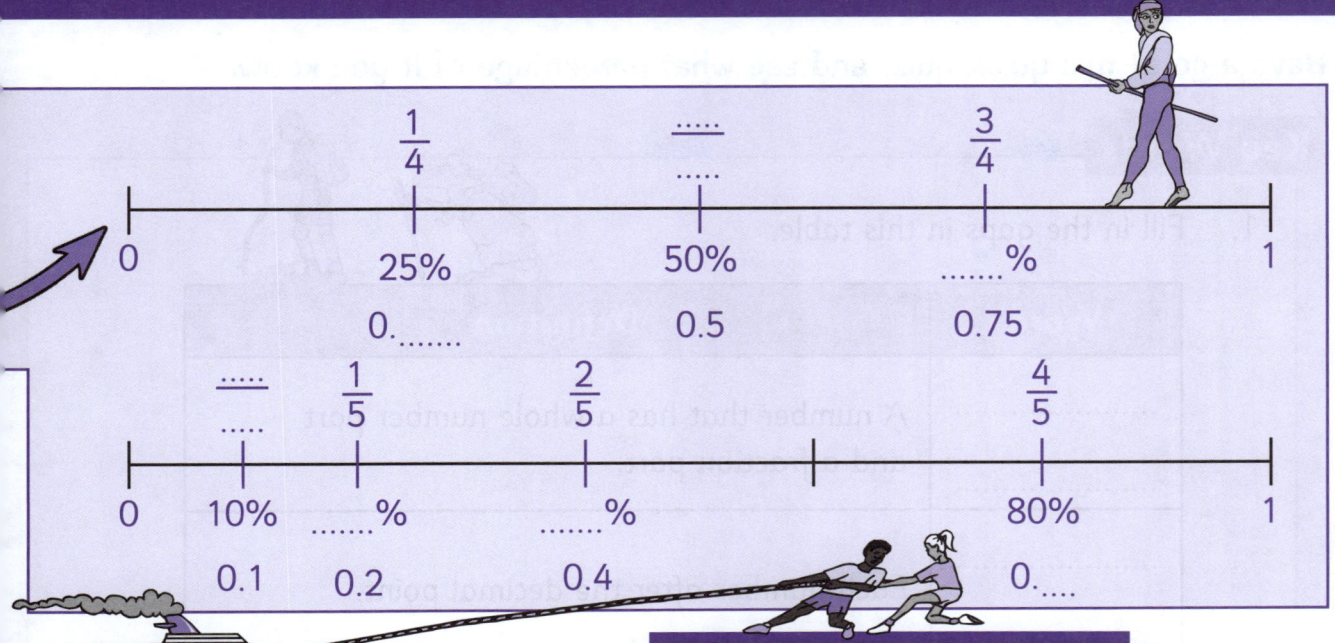

0 — 25% — 50% — ......% — 1

0....... 0.5 0.75

$\frac{\ldots}{\ldots}$ $\frac{1}{5}$ $\frac{2}{5}$ $\frac{4}{5}$

0 — 10% — ......% — ......% — 80% — 1

0.1 0.2 0.4 0.....

To convert a decimal to a percentage, ... by 100.

0.58 = 0.58 ... 100% = ... %

Move the digits 2 places to the .... to divide and 2 places to the .... to multiply.

Fractions and Decimals

To convert a fraction to a decimal:

Make an **e**.................. **f**..................

with 10, 100 or 1000 as the **d**...................

Then read off the number of **t**..............., **h**.................. or **t**...................

Now Try This

Write $3\frac{12}{30}$ as a decimal.

$\frac{12}{30}\overset{\div\ \ldots}{=}\frac{\ldots}{\ldots}$ This is .... **t**..............,
so $\frac{12}{30}$ is equivalent to ....

$3\frac{12}{30}$ = ... + ... = ...

Now Try This

Write $\frac{8}{25}$ as a decimal.

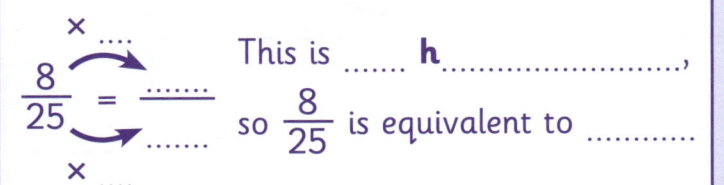

$\frac{8}{25}\overset{\times\ \ldots}{\underset{\times\ \ldots}{=}}\frac{\ldots}{\ldots}$ This is ...... **h**..................,
so $\frac{8}{25}$ is equivalent to ....

Fractions, Decimals & Percentages Quiz

Have a go at this quick quiz, and see what percentage of it you know.

Key Words

1. Fill in the gaps in this table.

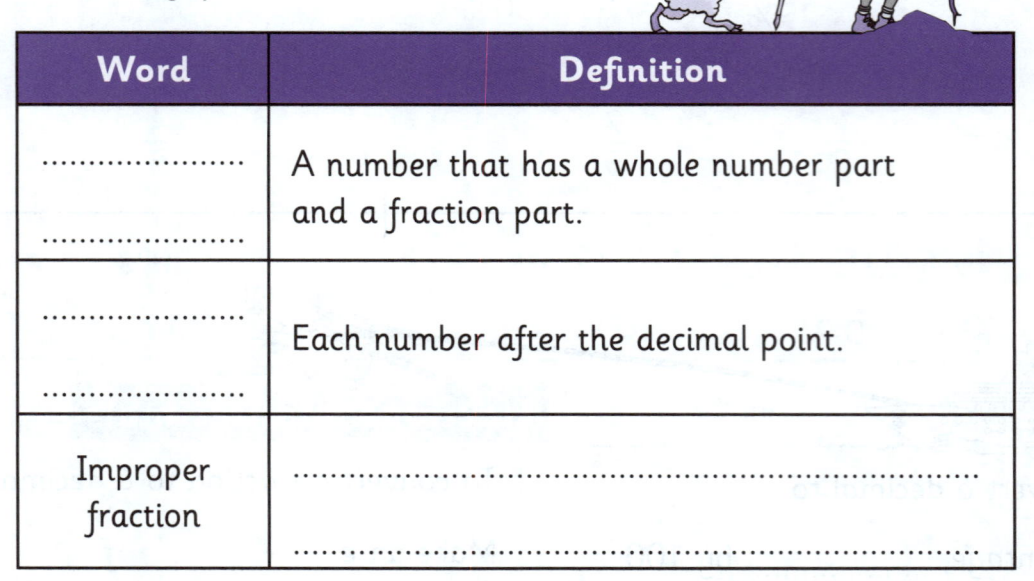

Word	Definition
....	A number that has a whole number part and a fraction part.
....	Each number after the decimal point.
Improper fraction	....

   3 marks

Key Diagrams

2. Fill in the missing decimals and percentages on this number line.

   Decimal: ....   Decimal: ....
   Percentage: ....   Percentage: ....

   Number line: 0 — $\frac{1}{4}$ — $\frac{1}{2}$ — $\frac{3}{4}$ — 1

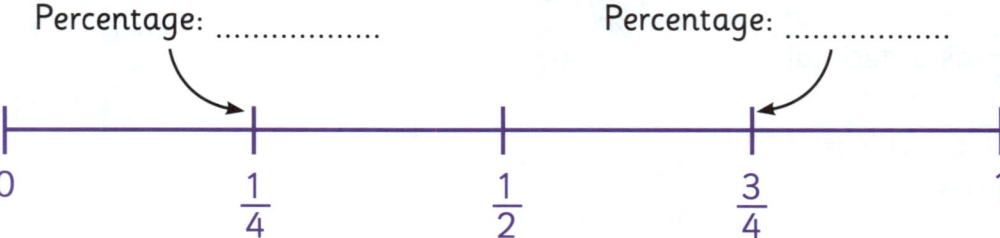

   4 marks

Now Try These

3. Which digit in 7.193 is in the hundredths place?

   ....

   1 mark

4. How do you convert a decimal to a percentage?

   ....

   1 mark

5. How do you add two fractions with the same denominator?

   ....

   1 mark

6. How do you find equivalent fractions?

   ....

   ....

   1 mark

7. Aisha wants to write some fractions with different denominators in order of size. She finds a common denominator. What should she do next?

   ....

   ....

   1 mark

8. What number should you use as the denominator when converting a percentage to a fraction?

   ....

   1 mark

9. Give the two steps you would do to multiply a whole number by a fraction.

   1. ....

   2. ....

   2 marks

Score:

Converting Units

Converting Metric Units

Multiply to go from a big unit to a smaller one.

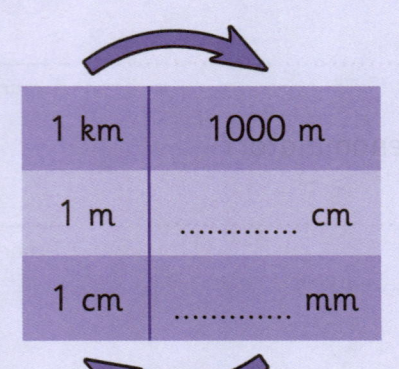

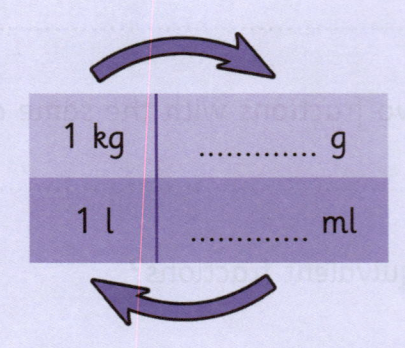

1 km	1000 m
1 m	.... cm
1 cm	.... mm

1 kg	.... g
1 l	.... ml

.... to go from a small unit to a bigger one.

Now Try This

An eagle has a mass of 4260 g. What is its mass in kilograms?

1 kg = ... g

So divide by .... :

4260 ÷ ....

= .... kg

Metric and Imperial Units

Metric units are used more than imperial units.

Type of unit: ....

- metres
- litres
- grams
- centimetres
- millilitres
- kilograms

Type of unit: ....

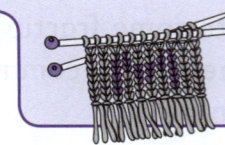

- miles
- feet
- pints
- inches
- pounds
- ounces

Converting Imperial Units

1 m	3 feet
8 km	5 miles
5 cm	2 inches

lengths

1 kg	2 pounds
100 g	4 ounces

1 l	2 pints

28 Measurement

Put measurements in the s.......... units before using them in calculations.

Now Try This

Jane is 1.3 m tall.
Tim is 22 cm shorter.
How tall is Tim?

Convert Jane's height into cm.

1 m = ... cm

So **m**............... by ....:

1.3 .... = ... cm

.... – .... = ... cm tall

Converting Units of Time

Now Try This

Eoin's birthday is 128 days away. How long is this in weeks and days?

1 week = ... days,

so work out 128 ÷ ....:

....) 1 2 8   .... r ....   So it's ...... weeks and .... days away.

Now Try This

A factory makes 4 toys every minute. How many toys does it make in 3 hours and 20 minutes?

1 hour = ... minutes,

so 3 hours = 3 × .... = ... minutes

.... + ... = ... minutes

.... × .... = ... toys

These are approximate conversions — they aren't exact. Write them using the sign ....:

5 cm .... 2 inches

Now Try This

Approximately how many ounces is 700 g? Use 100 g ≈ 4 ounces.

700 g ÷ .... g = ..., so 700 g is .... lots of .... g.

That's about .... lots of .... ounces.

So 700 g ≈ .... × .... ounces = ... ounces

Perimeter, Area and Volume

Finding Perimeters

To find the perimeter of a shape, ... up the .... of all of its sides.

If any side lengths are missing, use the other l................ to work them out.

Now Try This

What is the perimeter of this shape?

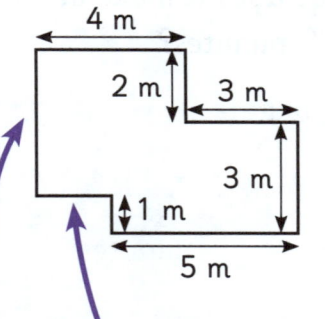

4 m
2 m *3 m*
3 m
1 m
5 m

Start by working out the two missing side lengths.

The total width is 4 + ... = ... m.
So this side is .... − .... = ... m.

The total length is 2 + ... = ... m.
So this side is .... − .... = ... m.

Add up all the sides to find the perimeter:
4 + 2 + ... + ... + ... + ... + ... + ... = ... m

Finding Areas

You can estimate the area of a shape on a grid by counting how many s................ and **half-s**................ it covers.

Now Try This

What is the area of this shape?
Each square has an area of 1 cm^2.

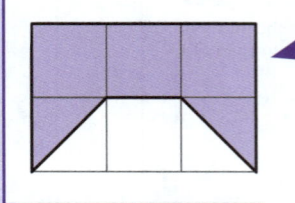

← It covers .... whole squares and .... half-squares.

Area = ... + $\frac{....}{....}$ + $\frac{....}{....}$

= ....

Finding Volumes

Volume: the amount of s............ a 3D object takes up.

Volume is measured in '............' units:

cm^3 is .... centimetres.

m^3 is ....

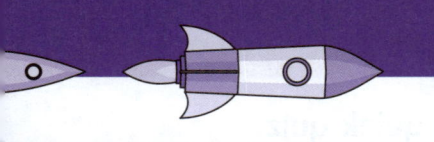

For more irregular shapes, count how many squares are more than .... covered.

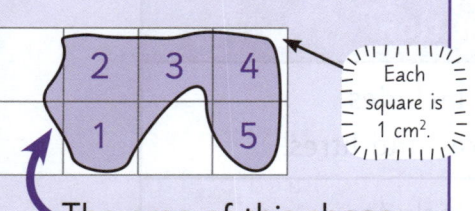

The area of this shape is about ....

Each square is 1 cm².

Area is usually measured in '...............' units:
cm² is .... centimetres.
m² is ....

Areas of Squares and Rectangles

To find the area of a square or rectangle, m............... the length by the width.

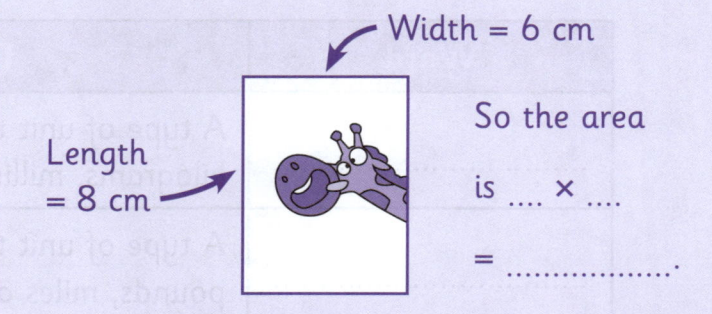

Width = 6 cm
Length = 8 cm

So the area is .... × ....
= ....

You can use this to work out missing sides.

Now Try This

A rectangular field has an area of 120 m². Its length is 12 m. What is its width?

Area = ... × width,

so 120 = ... × width

120 ÷ ...... = ..., so the width is ....

Now Try This

Find the volume of this cuboid. Each cube has a volume of 1 cm³.

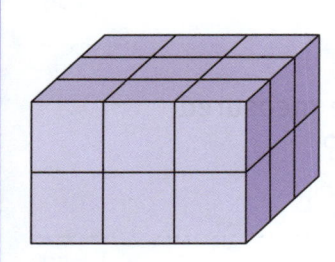

There are 2 layers of .... cubes each, so there are .... × 2 = ... cubes.

So the volume is ....

Capacity: the amount something can hold when it's f....... .

World's best mug

This can hold a maximum volume of 300 ml, so its capacity is 300 ml.

Measurement Quiz

Estimate your measurement knowledge by trying out this quick quiz.

Key Words

1. Fill in the gaps in this table.

Word	Definition
....	A type of unit that includes kilograms, millimetres and litres.
....	A type of unit that includes pounds, miles and pints.
Volume	....
....	The amount something can hold when it's full.

4 marks

Now Try These

2. True or false? To go from a small unit to a bigger one, you need to multiply. ....

1 mark

3. Calum is working out the area of a shape. Its sides are measured in centimetres. What units should he use in his answer?

....

1 mark

32 Measurement

4. How do you find the perimeter of a shape?

....

....

1 mark

5. How would you convert a time in hours to minutes?

....

1 mark

6. How do you work out the area of a rectangle from its length and width?

....

1 mark

7. What sign should you use to show that conversions are approximate? ....

1 mark

8. Each square on this grid has an area of 1 cm². Estimate the area of the purple shape.

....

1 mark

9. Fill in the missing numbers in these conversions.

a) 150 cm = ... m

b) 3.27 litres = ... ml

2 marks

Score:

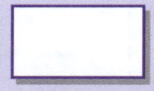

Angles

Angle Basics

Angles are measured in .... (°).   360°   ....°

Here are some important angles:

........°

Right angle   45° (half a
                               r............ angle)

Right angles are shown using a square.

Measuring and Drawing Angles

Use a protractor to measure and draw angles accurately.

The cross on the protractor needs to go where the two angle lines meet.

Now Try This

Measure the angle shown on the right.

1. Put the bottom line of your **p**........................ along one of the lines of the angle.

2. Read from the scale that has 0 on the line of your angle.

3. The angle is ....°.

Now Try This

Draw a 52° angle.

① Draw a line and line up the **p**........................ with it.

② Read around the scale from .... and mark where 52° is.

③ Join the end of the line to the mark. .... the angle.

34   Geometry

You can estimate other angles by comparing with these.

Now Try This

Estimate the size of this angle.

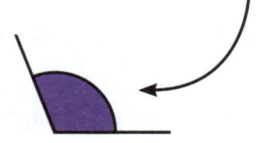

The angle is bigger than a r............. angle but smaller than one and a h........ right angles.

So ....° is a good estimate.

Types of Angle

Acute angles are .... than 90°.

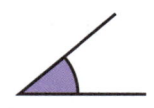

Obtuse angles are .... than 90° but .... than 180°.

.... angles are bigger than 180°.

Angle Rules

1 Angles around a point add up to ....°.

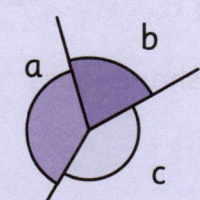

$a + b + c =$ ....°

2 Angles on a s................ l........ add up to ....°.

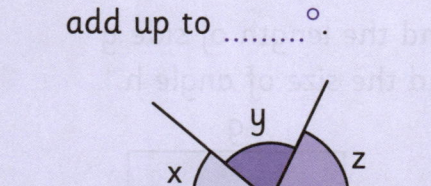

$x + y + z =$ ....°

3 Angles at a quarter turn add up to ......°.

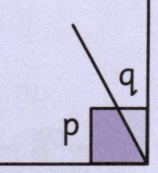

$p + q =$ ....°

Shapes

Regular and Irregular Polygons

A polygon is a 2D shape with straight ....

Regular polygon: all sides are the same l............ and all angles are the same s......... .

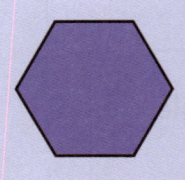

This shape has 6 equal sides and .... equal angles, so it is a r............ h............ .

Irregular polygon: does not have all s............ the same length and all a............ the same size.

This shape has .... sides, but they are not all the same l............, so it is an i............ P............ .

Properties of Rectangles

1. o............ sides of a rectangle are the same length.
2. All the angles in a rectangle are r............ angles.

Now Try This

Find the length of side g and the size of angle h.

g
3 cm
h
7 cm

Opposite sides are e............,
so g = ... cm

All angles are .... angles,
so h = ... °

Plans and Elevations

Plan: how a shape looks from directly a............ .

Elevation: how a shape looks from one s......... .

Elevations can be different depending on whether you're looking at the shape from the f............ or the s......... .

36   Geometry

3D Shapes and Nets

Cube

P.................
C.................

C.................

T.................
P.................

A **net** is a .... shape that you can f.......... to make a .... shape. Each shape in the net is a f.......... of the 3D shape. 3D shapes can have more than one net.

Cube:

Cuboid: Plan: Elevations:

(front)   (side)

Draw the missing diagrams in the empty boxes.

T.................
P...............:

Square-based pyramid: Plan: Elevation:

An arrow can be used to show the direction of the **e**...................

Cylinder: Plan: Elevation:

Triangular prism: Plan: Elevation:

Curved surfaces become flat 2D shapes in an elevation.

Coordinates & Transformations

Coordinates

Coordinates give the **p**............. of a point on a grid.

Read the ....-coordinate first, then the ....-coordinate.

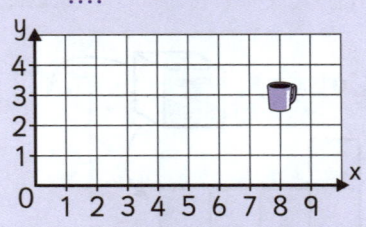

The coordinates of the mug are (...., ...).

Transformations

Transformation: a way of changing the **p**............. of a shape.

Reflections   **T**.............................

The shape doesn't change when it is reflected or ....

Reflections

Reflection: when a shape flips over a **m**............. line.

Its .... and shape don't change, and it doesn't **r**............. .

A point and its .... are always the same distance from the **m**............. line.

Now Try This

Reflect shape A in the horizontal mirror line.

Horizontal mirror line

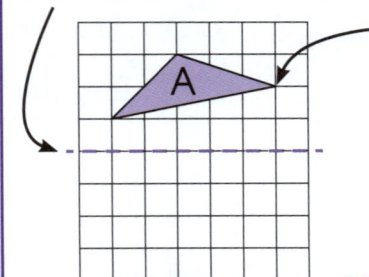

This point on A is .... units .... the mirror line.

So the reflected point will be .... units .... the mirror line.

Now Try This

Reflect shape B in the vertical mirror line.

Symmetry

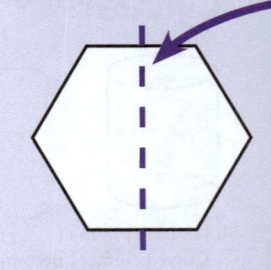

38   Geometry

Translations

Translation: when a shape slides from one position to another.

Its **s**......... and **s**............ don't change, and it doesn't rotate or flip over.

To translate a shape:

1 Pick a vertex. Move the correct number of squares, then mark a **c**............

2 Repeat for each **v**...............

3 Join up the **c**...............

This point on B is .... unit to the .... of the mirror line.

So it will be .... unit to the .... in the reflection.

— Vertical mirror line

Now Try This

Translate shape C 3 squares to the right and 6 squares down.

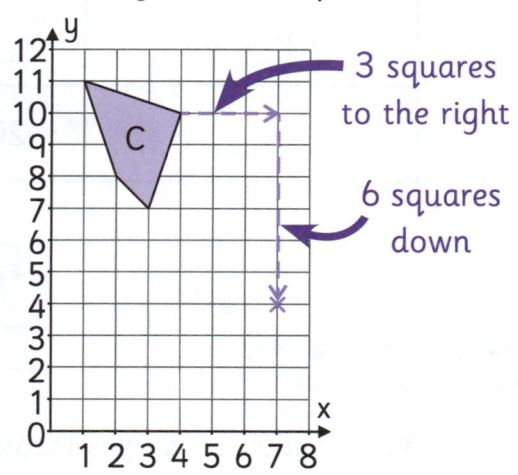

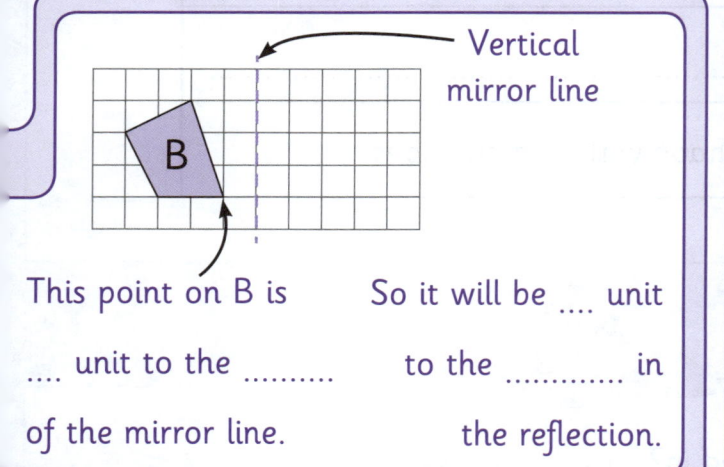

3 squares to the right

6 squares down

Line of Symmetry:

a .... drawn through a shape so that the shape is the .... on both sides of the line.

If you can do this, the shape is called symmetrical.

All .... polygons (and some .... ones) have lines of symmetry.

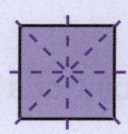

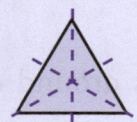

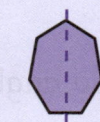

39

Geometry Quiz

Here's another quick quiz — let's see if you're angling for success...

Key Words

1. Fill in the blanks in this table.

Word	Definition
....	A mirror line drawn through a shape so that the shape is the same on both sides of the line.
Transformation	....
Elevation	....
....	A 2D shape with straight sides.

4 marks

Now Try These

2. What units are angles measured in?   ....

1 mark

3. What is the length of side a?

   .... cm

   4 cm   a
   10 cm

1 mark

4. What do angles around a point add up to?   ....°

1 mark

5. Is this angle acute, obtuse or reflex?

    ....

    1 mark

6. What is the first step to measuring an angle using a protractor?

    ....

    ....

    1 mark

7. Look at the shapes on the left.
    Circle all of the regular pentagons.

    1 mark

8. A point is 3 units to the right of a vertical mirror line.
    It is reflected in the mirror line. Where is the reflected point?

    ....

    1 mark

9. Look at the shape on the right.

    a) What is the name of this shape?

    ....

    b) What 2D shape is the plan of this shape?

    ....

    2 marks

10. Point P is translated 1 unit to
    the left and 3 units up. Which letter
    (W, X, Y or Z) shows the position
    of point P after the translation?   ....

    1 mark

    Score:

Line Graphs

Reading Off Line Graphs

Line graphs: show how something ....

To read information off a line graph:

1. Find the information you're given on one **a**.........

2. Go straight up or across to the line.

3. Move across or down to the other .... and read off the value.

Now Try This

This line graph shows the ticket sales at a cinema over four days.

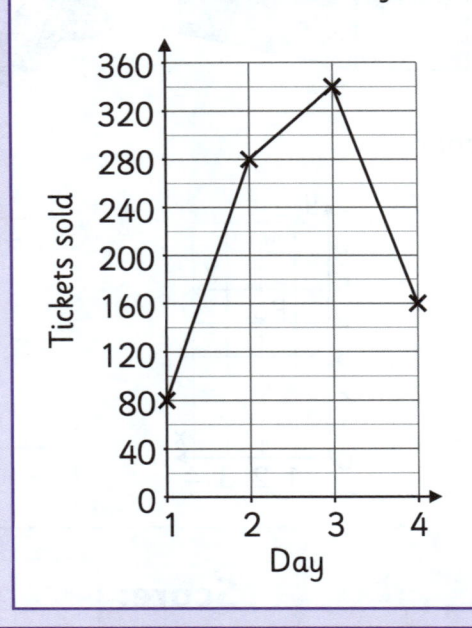

How many tickets were sold on day 2?

Start at day 2 on the horizontal axis.

.... tickets were sold on day 2.

On which day were 340 tickets sold?

Start at 340 on the vertical axis.

340 tickets were sold on day ..... .

Line Graph Problems

You can find out information from line graphs.

Now Try This

This graph shows sales of apples at a shop over five days.

How many apples were sold in total on Thursday and Friday?

Find Thursday and read up:

.... apples were sold.

Find Friday and read up:

.... apples were sold.

So .... + ... = ... apples were sold in total on Thursday and Friday.

42   Statistics

> To find totals, read off the values and .... them together.

To find differences, read off the values and .... them.

Now Try This

This line graph shows the number of children at a park one day.

How many more children were at the park at 3 pm than at 11 am?

Read up from the '............' axis:

At 11 am, there were ...... children.

At 3 pm, there were ...... children.

...... − ...... = ... more children were at the park at 3 pm.

Comparing Line Graphs

You can compare two line graphs on the same axes.

This graph shows how far Maya and Clare ran in 10 minutes.

After 2 minutes, Maya had run .... km, and Clare had run .... km.

To run 1.5 km, it took Maya ...... minutes and Clare ...... minutes.

The .... tells you what each line represents.

Tables

Reading Off Tables

Tables are often used to show data.

Read off information by finding the correct **r**....... and **c**.................

This table shows the number of hot drinks sold by a cafe one weekend.

	Saturday	Sunday
Tea	10	16
Coffee	25	14
Hot choc	15	10

.... cups of coffee were sold on Saturday.

Completing Tables

To **complete** a table, use the information you're given to find the **missing** numbers.

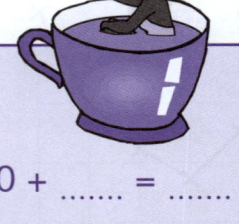

10 + ... = ... cups of tea were sold in total.

16 + ... + ... = ... hot drinks were sold on Sunday.

Reading Timetables

Timetables show when things are happening. Here is part of a bus timetable:

Each **c**............... shows the times for one bus.

The 09:50 bus from the Town Centre gets to Park Avenue at ....

Town Centre	09:10	09:50	10:45
Market Street	09:15	09:55	10:50
Park Avenue	09:22	10:02	10:57
Sports Centre	09:30	10:10	11:05

The journey from the Town Centre to the Sports Centre takes

+ 5
+ ....
+ ....

5 + ... + ... = ... minutes.

44   Statistics

Now Try This

40 people chose their favourite pet from the list in the table.
Two more people chose dog than chose rabbit. Half as many people chose hamster as chose cat. Use this information to complete the table.

Pet	Number of people
Cat	12
Dog	?
Rabbit	8
Hamster	?
Fish	?

...... people chose rabbit,

so ...... + ... = ... people chose dog.

...... people chose cat,

so ...... ÷ ...... = ... people chose hamster.

The rest of the people chose fish,

so subtract from the total:

...... – 12 – ...... – 8 – .... = ... people chose fish.

Timetable Problems

Use timetables to solve problems.

Now Try This

Jack lives in Mouseley. He needs to be in Rodentonia by 2:50 pm. Which train should he catch?

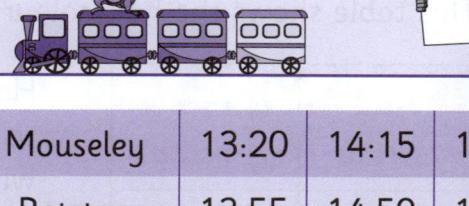

Mouseley	13:20	14:15	15:00
Ratston	13:55	14:50	15:35
Rodentonia	14:04	14:59	15:44

1 Find the r........ for Rodentonia and read across.

2 2:50 pm is the same as .... The last time before .... is ....

3 Read up the .... to Mouseley. Jack should catch the .... train.

Statistics Quiz

It's statistically very likely that there is a quiz on this page. Oh look!

Key Words

1. Fill in the blanks in this table.

Word	Definition
Line graph	....
....	A way of showing data using rows and columns.
....	A chart that shows when things are happening.

3 marks

Now Try These

2. This table shows the hair colour of the 32 pupils in Ryan's class.

Hair colour	Number of pupils
Brown	14
Blonde	9
Black	5
Red	?

How could you use the table to calculate the number of pupils with red hair?

....
....
....

1 mark

46   Statistics

3. How would you find the difference between two values on a line graph?

....

1 mark

4. Dunja wants to know which bus to catch to get to Circle Green by 11:20.
She looks at the timetable below and finds the row for Circle Green. What is the next step?

The Square	10:20	10:45	11:05
Rhombus Hill	10:35	11:00	11:20
Circle Green	10:48	11:13	11:33

....

....

1 mark

5. This line graph shows the number of push-ups Kane did over four days.

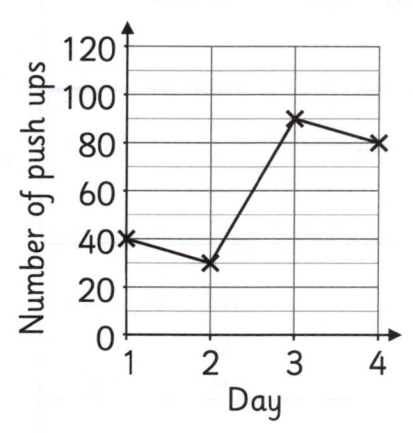

a) On which day did Kane do 90 push-ups?

Day ....

b) Complete the calculation to work out how many push-ups Kane did in total on days 1 and 2.

40 + ... = ... push ups

2 marks

Score:

End of Year Quiz

That's almost it for this book — but before you go, here's one more quiz...

Key Words

1. Fill in the blanks in this table.

Word	Definition
....	Numbers that are less than zero.
....	The amount of space a 3D object takes up.
Regular polygon	....
....	A type of graph that shows how something changes.
....	A number that has exactly two factors: 1 and itself.
Square number	....
Acute angle	....
....	A number that is a factor of two (or more) numbers.

8 marks

2. Write down the definitions of the following words.

   a) Plan: ....

   b) Elevation: ....

   c) Net: ....

   ....

   3 marks

3. Match each word to the correct definition.

Improper fraction	A fraction that looks different to another fraction, but is equal to it.
Mixed number	A fraction where the numerator is bigger than the denominator.
Equivalent fraction	A number that has a whole number part and a fraction part.

   2 marks

4. Use the words in the box below to fill in the blanks.

   reflection   translation   mirror   position

   Transformation: A way of changing the .... of a shape.

   .... : When a shape slides from one position to another.

   .... : When a shape flips over a .... line.

   4 marks

Now Try These

5. Circle the number below that is not a multiple of 6.

   12   48   24   32   18

   1 mark

6. Look at the shape on the right.
   Is it regular or irregular?

   ....

   1 mark

7. What is the sum of angles in a quarter turn? ....°

   1 mark

8. Which digit in 836 201 is in the ten thousands place? ....

   1 mark

9. How would you compare two fractions
   that have the same denominator?

   ....

   1 mark

10. What is the size of the marked angle?

    ....°

    1 mark

11. What number would you multiply by to convert
    a distance in centimetres into millimetres?

    ....

    1 mark

12. 46% of people asked in a survey said they
    like broccoli. What percentage of the people
    in the survey didn't say they like broccoli? ....%

    1 mark

50   End of Year Quiz

13. How many thousandths are equivalent to 1 tenth?

.... 1 mark

14. True or false? A 3D shape only has one possible net.

.... 1 mark

15. When using Roman numerals, how would you read a smaller numeral before a bigger one?

....

1 mark

16. When dividing a number by 100, how do the digits move?

....

1 mark

17. Write the improper fractions below as mixed numbers.

   a) $\frac{13}{9}$ = ...   b) $\frac{15}{4}$ = ...

2 marks

18. Bandile is thinking of a prime number. It doesn't end in 1, 3, 7 or 9. What number could he be thinking of?

.... or ....

1 mark

19. This cuboid is made of 1 cm³ cubes. What is the volume of the cuboid?

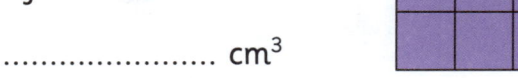

.... cm³

1 mark

20. When subtracting using columns, which place value column do you subtract first?

....

1 mark

21. 40 people chose their favourite sandwich filling and type of bread. The results are shown in this table.

	White	Brown
Cheese	12	7
Ham	5	4
Chicken	3	7

   a) How many people chose a cheese sandwich? ....

   b) How many people chose brown bread? ....

   2 marks

22. What is the first step to subtract two fractions with different denominators?

   ....

   1 mark

23. Amy wants to work out 39 × 7 in her head. What calculations could she do instead to make it easier?

   ....

   1 mark

24. Look at the shape on the right.

   a) What is the length of side a?

   .... cm

   b) What is the perimeter of the shape?

   .... cm

   2 marks

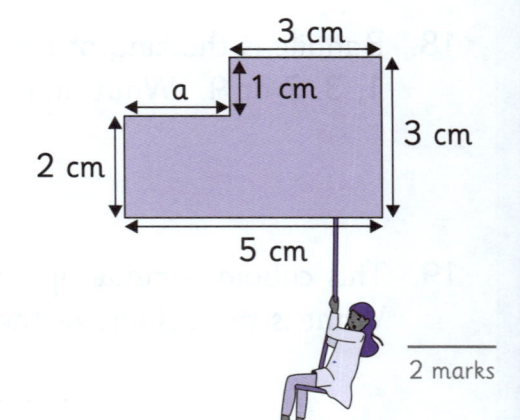

25. Using the conversion 1 kg ≈ 2 pounds, convert:

   a) 5 kg into pounds   .... pounds

   b) 20 pounds into kilograms   .... kg

   2 marks

End of Year Quiz

26. The line graph on the right shows the number of blackbirds and sparrows that Penny saw in three days.

   a) How many blackbirds did she see on Day 2? ....

   b) How many more sparrows did she see than blackbirds on Day 3? ....

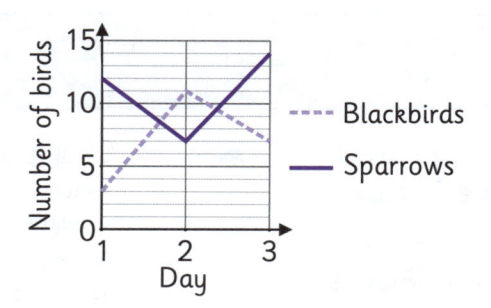

   2 marks

27. Eleri thinks of a 3D shape. Its plan is a square and all of its elevations are triangles. What 3D shape is she thinking of?

   ....

   1 mark

28. Point X is reflected in the horizontal mirror line. Which letter (A, B or C) shows the position of the reflected point?

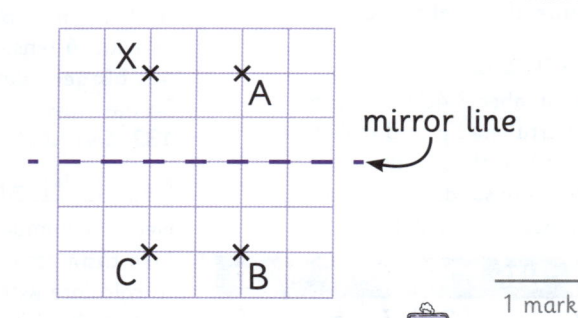

   ....

   1 mark

29. This is part of a bus timetable.

   a) How long does it take the 16:09 bus from Apple Road to get to Grape Street?

   .... minutes

Apple Road	15:01	15:38	16:09
Lime Lane	15:11	15:48	16:19
Grape Street	15:27	16:04	16:35
Pear Avenue	15:50	16:27	16:58

   b) Ishaan needs to be at Pear Avenue by 4:45 pm. What time is the latest bus he could catch from Lime Lane?

   .... : ....

   2 marks

Score:

Answers

Number and Place Value

Pages 2-3 — Number Basics

Place Value

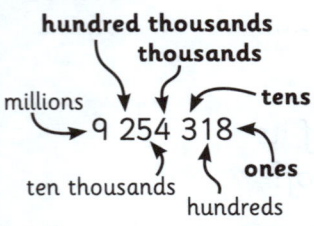

```
            hundred thousands
                    thousands
millions              ↓  ↓   tens
      → 9 254 318 ←
          ↑  ↑      ones
ten thousands
            hundreds
```

nine million, **two hundred** and **fifty-four thousand**, **three hundred** and **eighteen**.

Partitioning

The number 3 487 502 can be partitioned into 3 millions, **4** hundred thousands, **8** ten thousands, **7** thousands, **5** hundreds and **2** ones.

M	HTh	TTh	Th	H	T	O
3	4	8	7	5	0	2

There aren't any **tens**.

3 487 502 = 3 000 000 + 400 000 + 80 000 + **7**000 + **5**00 + **2**

Diagram: **2500**

3 487 502 = 3 400 000 + 85 000 + **2500** + 2

Comparing and Ordering

> means "is greater than".
< means "is less than".

Ascending order: numbers go from **smallest** to **biggest**.
Descending order: numbers go from biggest to smallest.

Both numbers have **3** hundred thousands.
2 is **greater** than 0.
So 325 604 **>** 305 624

1051 is the only number with a **thousands** digit, so it's the **biggest**.
211 has 2 hundreds, 132 and 141 have **1** hundred. 2 is **bigger** than 1, so 211 is next **biggest**.
141 has **4** tens, 132 has **3** tens.
4 is **bigger** than 3, so **141** is bigger.
So the order is
132, **141**, **211**, **1051**.

Negative Numbers

Negative numbers are numbers **less than** zero. Use **number lines** to calculate with them.
To find the difference between two numbers, count the **places** between them.

Between −3 and 0 there are **3** places. Between 0 and 5 there are **5** places.
So the difference is **3 + 5 = 8**.

To add, find your starting point and count **on**. To subtract, find your starting point and count **back**.

1 Start at **−1**.
2 Count **back** 10 places.
3 Then count back **2** places.
−1 − 12 = **−13**

Pages 4-5 — Powers of 10 and Rounding

Counting in Powers of 10

Power of 10: a **1** followed by zeros.
E.g. 10, 100, **1000**, **10 000**, etc.

To count on in steps of a power of 10, add **1** to the digit matching the power.

To count on from 25 384 in steps of 100, add 1 to the **hundreds** digit each time.
25 **4**84   25 **5**84

To count on in steps of 10 000, add 1 to the **ten thousands** digit each time.

To count back in steps of a power of 10, subtract **1** from the digit matching the power.
1**7** 324   1**6** 324   1**5** 324

Rounding Whole Numbers

2 Look at the digit to the **right** of the place being rounded to — the decider.
3 If the decider is less than **5**, then round **down**. If the decider is **5 or more**, then round up.

2067 is between 20**6**0 and 20**7**0.
The decider is **7**
7 is more than 5, so round 2067 **up** to **2070**.

Answers

Multiplying by 10, 100, 1000

To multiply by 10, move all the digits **1** place to the **left**.
51 × 10 = **510**

To multiply by 100, move all the digits **2** places to the **left**.
51 × 100 = **5100**

To multiply by 1000, move all the digits **3** places to the **left**.
51 × 1000 = **51 000**

32.8 × 1000 = **32 800**

| 3 | 2 | 8 | 0 | 0 | . | | |

Move all the digits **3** places to the **left**.

Fill spaces before the decimal point with **zeros**.

Dividing by 10, 100, 1000

To divide by 10, move all the digits **1** place to the **right**.
350 ÷ 10 = **35**

To divide by 100, move all the digits **2** places to the **right**.
350 ÷ 100 = **3.5**

To divide by 1000, move all the digits **3** places to the **right**.
350 ÷ 1000 = **0.35**

The number of **zeros** tells you how many **places** to move the digits.

6.3 ÷ 100 = **0.063**

| 0 | . | 0 | 6 | 3 |

Fill space before the decimal point with a **zero**.

Move all the digits **2** places to the **right**.

Fill the space between the decimal point and the first digit with **zeros**.

Pages 6-7 — Number Facts

Multiples

Multiples of a number: the numbers in its times table. E.g. the multiples of 7 are 7, **14**, **21**, **28**, etc.

Multiples of 2: End in **even** numbers or **0**

Multiples of 5: End in **0** or **5**

Multiples of 10: End in **0**

Common multiple of two numbers: a number that is a **multiple** of **both** numbers.

First few multiples of 8:
8   **16**   **24**   32

First few multiples of 12:
12   24   36   **48**

24 is a common multiple of 8 and 12.

Factors

Factors of a number: **whole numbers** that **divide** exactly into it.

Factors come in **pairs** that **multiply** together to give the number.

If there's an **odd** number of factors, the middle factor multiplies by itself.

12:   1 × 12   2 × 6   3 × 4

The factor pairs are 1 and **12**, **2** and 6, and 3 and **4**.

Common factor of two numbers: a number that is a **factor** of **both** numbers.

Factors of 15: **1**   **3**   **5**   15
Factors of 27: 1   **3**   **9**   27

1 and **3** are the **common factors** of 15 and 27.

Square and Cube Numbers

Square number: the number you get when you multiply a number by **itself**.

4 × 4 = 4 squared = 4^2 = **16**
6 × 6 = 6 squared = 6^2 = **36**
9 × 9 = 9 squared = 9^2 = **81**

Square numbers are the **areas** in this pattern of squares.

1 × 1 = **1**
2 × 2 = **4**
3 × 3 = **9**

Cube number: the number you get when you multiply a number by itself **twice**.

2 × 2 × 2 = 2 cubed = 2^3 = **8**
4 × 4 × 4 = 4 cubed = 4^3 = **64**
5 × 5 × 5 = 5 cubed = 5^3 = **125**

Cube numbers are the **volumes** in this pattern of cubes.

1 × 1 × 1 = **1**
2 × 2 × 2 = **8**
3 × 3 × 3 = **27**

Roman Numerals

Roman numerals are letters that represent **numbers**.

V = **5**   X = **10**
C = **100**   D = **500**

1 **Add** together numerals that are the same.
   III = **3**

2 Smaller numeral before a **bigger** one — subtract.
   IX = **9**

3 Smaller numeral **after** a bigger one — **add**.
   MC = **1100**.

50 + 10 + **10** = **70**
10 − 1 = **9**
70 + **9** = **79**

Answers

Pages 8-9 — Prime Numbers

Prime Numbers

Prime number: has exactly two **factors** — **1** and **itself**.

A number with more than two **factors** is called a composite number.

1. **1** is not a prime number — it only has 1 factor.
2. All prime numbers end in 1, 3, **7** or **9**, except for **2** and **5**.
3. **2** is the only even prime number.

The prime numbers below 20 are: 2, **3**, 5, **7**, **11**, 13, 17 and **19**.

Prime Factors

1. Write down any **factor pair** of the number.
2. Split composite numbers into **factor pairs**.
3. Repeat until all the factors are **prime**.

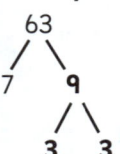

```
    63
   /  \
  7    9
      / \
     3   3
```

7 is a **prime** number.
Split **9** into a factor pair.
63 = 7 × **3** × **3**, so the prime numbers are **3**, **3** and 7.

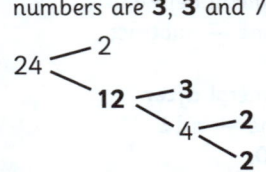

```
       2
24 — 
       12 — 3
            4 — 2
                2
```

Split **12** into a factor pair.
24 = 2 × **3** × 4
3 is a prime number.
All of the factors are prime numbers, so the prime factors of 24 are **2** and **3**.

Checking if a Number is Prime

1. Does the number end in 1, 3, **7** or **9**?
2. Does it have exactly two **factors**? Is the number **2** or **5**?

27, 53, 49, and 31 end in a 1, 3, 7 or 9, so could be **prime**.
Factors of 27: **1, 3, 9** and **27**
Factors of 53: **1** and **53**
Factors of 49: **1, 7** and **49**
Factors of 31: **1** and **31**
So **53** and **31** are prime numbers.

Pages 10-11 — Number and Place Value Quiz

Key Words

1. Factor: **A whole number that divides exactly into a number.**
   Cube number: **The number you get when you multiply a number by itself twice.**
   Common multiple: **A number that is a multiple of two (or more) numbers.**
   (1 mark for each)

Now Try These

2. **0** or **5** (1 mark for each)
3. 7 **ten thousands**, 1 **thousand**, 3 hundreds, 2 **tens** and 6 **ones**. (1 mark for each)
4. "is less than" (1 mark)
5. 20   5   42   ㊱   8 (1 mark)
6. Subtract 1 from the digit matching the power. (1 mark)
7. a) 5 (1 mark)
   b) Up (1 mark)
8. 3 places to the left (1 mark)
9. 21 has more than two factors (1, 3 , 7 and 21). (1 mark)
10. 1000 (1 mark)
11. Split 6 into another factor pair. (1 mark)

Calculations

Pages 12-13 — Adding and Subtracting

Adding in Columns

1. Add the **ones** column.

    ```
       TTh Th  H  T  O
        6  2   8  3  2
    +   1  3   7  9  5
    ─────────────────
                     7
    ```

2. Add the **tens** column.

    ```
       TTh Th  H  T  O
        6  2   8  3  2
    +   1  3   7  9  5
    ─────────────────
                  2  7
                1
    ```

    3 + **9** = **12**, so put **2** in the **tens** column and carry **1** to the **hundreds** column.

3. Add the **hundreds** column.

    ```
       TTh Th  H  T  O
        6  2   8  3  2
    +   1  3   7  9  5
    ─────────────────
               6  2  7
             1 1
    ```

    8 + 7 + 1 = **16**, so put **6** in the **hundreds** column and carry **1** to the **thousands** column.

    ```
       TTh Th  H  T  O
        6  2   8  3  2
    +   1  3   7  9  5
    ─────────────────
        7  6   6  2  7
             1 1
    ```

    So 62 832 + 13 795 = **76 627**

Answers

Subtracting in Columns

```
  H T O . t
  8 3 5 . 3
- 5 1 6 . 2
          .1
```

2. Subtract the **tenths**: 3 − 2 = **1**
3. Subtract the **ones**. You can't do **5** − **6**, so exchange 1 ten for 10 ones. Then **15** − **6** = **9**.

```
  H T²O¹. t
  8 3̸ 5̸. 3
- 5 1 6 . 2
        9.1
```

4. Subtract the **tens**: 2 − 1 = **1**
Then the **hundreds**: 8 − 5 = **3**

```
  H T²O¹. t
  8 3̸ 5̸. 3
- 5 1 6 . 2
  3 1 9 . 1
```

So 835.3 − 516.2 = **319.1**

Addition and Subtraction Problems

Max had £7.50 + £5.95 = **£13.45**
Now Max has
£13.45 − £10.40 = **£3.05**

Mental Calculations

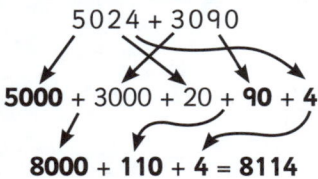

5024 + 3090

5000 + 3000 + 20 + **90** + 4

8000 + 110 + 4 = **8114**

Multiply both numbers by **10** to get whole numbers: 93 − **48** = **45**
Adjust by dividing by **10**:
9.3 − 4.8 = **45** ÷ **10** = **4.5**

Checking Answers

You can use rounding to **estimate** answers.
To the nearest whole number, 38.9 rounds to **39** and 17.3 rounds to **17**.
39 − 17 = 22
This is not close to **31.6**, so Li is wrong.

Pages 14-15 — Multiplying and Dividing

Long Multiplication

Partition the 2-digit number.
Multiply by each part separately.
Then **add** together.

1 Find 2317 × **3**.
3 × 7 = **21**, so put the **1** in the **ones** column and carry **2** to the **tens** column.
3 × 10 = **30**, plus the carried **20** is **50**.

2 Find 2317 × **20**.
20 × 7 = **140**, so put **4** and **0** in the correct columns and carry **1** to the **hundreds** column.
20 × 10 = **200**, plus the carried **100** is **300**.

3 **Add** the answers together.

```
    2 3 1 7
  ×     2 3
    6 9 5 1
  4 6 3 4 0
  5 3 2 9 1
    1 1
```

2317 × 23 = 6951 + 46 340
         = **53 291**

Written Division

```
        9
  5 ) 4 6 ¹8 2
```

5 × 9 = **45**, so 5 goes into 46 **nine** times with **1** left over.

```
        9 3
  5 ) 4 6 ¹8 ³2
```

5 × 3 = **15**, so 5 goes into 18 **three** times with **3** left over.

```
        9 3 6  r 2
  5 ) 4 6 ¹8 ³2
```

5 × 6 = **30**, so 5 goes into 32 **six** times with **2** left over.
So 4682 ÷ 5 = **936** remainder **2**.
The remainder can be written as a **fraction** → 936 $\frac{2}{5}$
or as a **decimal**. → **936.4**

Mental Calculations

Tony swims 28 × 6 lengths in total.
28 = 30 − **2**, so work out
30 × 6 and **2** × 6, then subtract:
30 × 6 = **180** and 2 × 6 = **12**
He swims **180** − **12** = **168** lengths.
114 = 60 + **54**
So work out 60 ÷ 6 and **54** ÷ 6, then add the answers together:
60 ÷ 6 = **10** and 54 ÷ 6 = **9**
So 114 ÷ 6 = **10** + **9** = **19**.

Wordy Problems

Anil spent £8 × 3 = **£24**.
So Cleo spent **£24** ÷ **4** = **£6**.

Answers

Pages 16-17 — Calculations Quiz

Key Words

1. **Remainder**: The amount that is left over after a division.
   Estimating: A way to check answers, e.g. by rounding.
   (1 mark for each)

Now Try These

2. 1. as a fraction (1 mark)
   2. as a decimal (1 mark)
3. 42 + 30 = 72. This isn't close to 64.2, so the answer is wrong. (1 mark)
4. Do the whole-number calculation, then adjust the answer by dividing it by 10. (1 mark)
5. Exchange 1 ten for 10 ones, then do 12 − 6. (1 mark)
6. a) 10 and 8 (1 mark for both)
   b) Add the two answers together. (1 mark)
7. a) Ones (1 mark)
   b) Carry the 1 to the thousands column. (1 mark)
8. a) 6 (1 mark)
   b) 3 (1 mark)

Fractions, Decimals & Percentages

Pages 18-19 — Fractions

Equivalent Fractions

Equivalent fractions look different, but are **equal**.

2 parts out of **4** are shaded, so $\frac{2}{4}$ is shaded.

1 part out of **2** is shaded, so $\frac{1}{2}$ is shaded.

The **same** amount of each circle is shaded, so $\frac{2}{4}$ is **equivalent** to $\frac{1}{2}$.

To find equivalent fractions, **multiply** or **divide** the numerator and denominator by the **same** number.

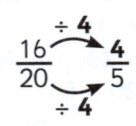

$$\frac{2}{3} \xrightarrow{\times 5} \frac{10}{15} \qquad \frac{16}{20} \xrightarrow{\div 4} \frac{4}{5}$$

1 tenth is equivalent to **10** hundredths.

$$\frac{7}{10} \xrightarrow{\times 10} \frac{70}{100}$$

Improper Fractions and Mixed Numbers

improper fraction: a fraction where the numerator is **bigger** than the denominator

mixed number: has a **whole number** part and a **fraction** part

Fractions where the numerator is smaller than the denominator are called "**proper fractions**".

$\frac{12}{7}$ is the same as $1\frac{5}{7}$

12 sevenths

1 whole and 12 − 7 = **5** sevenths

$2\frac{3}{8}$ is the same as $\frac{19}{8}$

2 wholes = **16** eighths.
Plus **3** eighths
19 eighths

Ordering Fractions

If the fractions have the same denominator, compare the **numerators**.

Fractions with bigger **numerators** are **bigger**.

1 Find a **common denominator**.
2 Write all the fractions as equivalent fractions using the **common denominator**.
3 Compare the **numerators**.

24 is a common multiple of 8, 4 and 12, so make this the **denominator**.

$$\frac{3}{8} \xrightarrow{\times 3} \frac{9}{24}$$

$$\frac{1}{4} \xrightarrow{\times 6} \frac{6}{24}$$

$$\frac{5}{12} \xrightarrow{\times 2} \frac{10}{24}$$

From smallest to largest, the order is $\frac{6}{24}, \frac{9}{24}, \frac{10}{24}$.

Change the fractions back to the ones in the question:
$\frac{1}{4}, \frac{3}{8}, \frac{5}{12}$

Answers

Pages 20-21 — Fraction Calculations

Adding and Subtracting — Same Denominator

When fractions have the same denominator, add or subtract the **numerators**.

Add the **numerators**:
$$\frac{5}{11} + \frac{8}{11} = \frac{5+8}{11} = \frac{13}{11}$$
You can also write this as $1\frac{2}{11}$.

Add and subtract the **numerators**:
$$\frac{18}{13} - \frac{9}{13} + \frac{3}{13} = \frac{18-9+3}{13} = \frac{12}{13}$$

Adding and Subtracting — Different Denominators

You can only add or subtract fractions if they have the **same** denominator.

Find **equivalent** fractions that have a **common denominator**.

Add or subtract the **numerators**.

18 is a common multiple of 6 and 9, so make 18 the **denominator**.

$$\frac{5}{6} \xrightarrow{\times 3} \frac{15}{18} \qquad \frac{4}{9} \xrightarrow{\times 2} \frac{8}{18}$$

$$\frac{5}{6} + \frac{4}{9} = \frac{15}{18} + \frac{8}{18} = \frac{15+8}{18} = \frac{23}{18}$$

Change mixed numbers to **improper fractions** before adding or subtracting them.

$$1\frac{3}{10} = \frac{10}{10} + \frac{3}{10} = \frac{13}{10}$$

30 is a common multiple of 10 and 15, so use **30** as the common denominator.

$$\frac{13}{10} \xrightarrow{\times 3} \frac{39}{30} \qquad \frac{8}{15} \xrightarrow{\times 2} \frac{16}{30}$$

$$1\frac{3}{10} - \frac{8}{15} = \frac{39}{30} - \frac{16}{30} = \frac{23}{30}$$

Multiplying Fractions

To multiply a whole number by a fraction, divide by the **denominator** and multiply by the **numerator**.

When you're dealing with fractions, "of" means "**times**".

Divide by the **denominator**:
$36 \div 9 = 4$
Multiply by the **numerator**:
$4 \times 2 = 8$
So $\frac{2}{9}$ of $36 = 8$

$2\frac{3}{4} = 2 + \frac{3}{4}$

Work out 2×8: $2 \times 8 = 16$
$\frac{1}{4} \times 8 = 8 \div 4 = 2$,
so $\frac{3}{4} \times 8 = 2 \times 3 = 6$.
So $2\frac{3}{4} \times 8 = 16 + 6 = 22$

Pages 22-23 — Decimals

Tenths, Hundredths and Thousandths

Decimals are a way to write a number that isn't a **whole number**.

The first few places after the decimal point are the **tenths**, **hundredths** and thousandths.

$$4\underset{\text{4 ones}}{.}\underset{\text{5 tenths}}{5}\underset{\text{3 hundredths}}{3}\underset{\text{7 thousandths}}{7}$$

0.1 = one **tenth** = $\frac{1}{10}$

0.01 = one hundredth = $\frac{1}{100}$

0.001 = one thousandth = $\frac{1}{1000}$

1 tenth = **100** thousandths
1 **hundredth** = 10 thousandths

Rounding Decimals

Each number after the decimal point is called a **decimal place** (d.p.).

1. Count the number of **decimal places** you need to keep.
2. Look at the next digit to the **right** — the decider.
3. If the decider is less than **5**, round **down**. If the decider is **5 or more**, round **up**.

You need to keep 1 decimal place, so the decider is the **hundredths** digit.

7 is bigger than 5, so round 4.57 **up** to **4.6**.

Answers

Writing Decimals as Fractions

$0.7 = 7$ **tenths** $= \frac{7}{10}$

$0.19 = 19$ **hundredths** $= \frac{19}{100}$

This has **103** thousandths.
So the fraction is $\frac{103}{1000}$.

This has **2** ones and **81** thousandths.
You can write this as a mixed number: $2\frac{81}{1000}$

Ordering Decimals

To put decimals in order, look at the digits in each **place value** column.

If the digits in one column are the **same**, compare the digits in the next column.

0.579	0.579	0.579	**0.572**
1.340	**0.600**	**0.572**	**0.579**
0.600	0.572	**0.600**	0.600
0.572	**1.340**	1.340	1.340

From smallest to largest:
0.572, 0.579, 0.6, 1.34

Pages 24-25 — Fractions, Decimals & Percentages

Percentage Basics

"Per cent" means "out of **100**".
% is a short way of writing per cent, so 40% means "**40** out of **100**".
100% is the total amount.

The total is **100**%.
So **100**% − **23**% = **77**% don't have blue eyes.

Common Conversions

You can write percentages as **decimals** or **fractions**.

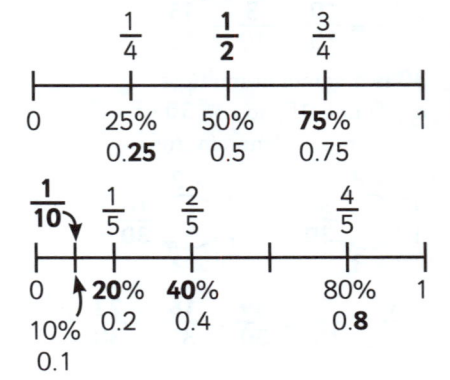

Number line: 0 — $\frac{1}{4}$ (25%, 0.25) — $\frac{1}{2}$ (50%, 0.5) — $\frac{3}{4}$ (**75%**, 0.75) — 1

Number line: 0 — $\frac{1}{10}$ (10%, 0.1) — $\frac{1}{5}$ (**20%**, 0.2) — $\frac{2}{5}$ (**40%**, 0.4) — $\frac{4}{5}$ (80%, 0.8) — 1

Percentages and Fractions

1 Put the percentage as the **numerator**.

$67\% = \frac{67}{100}$

2 Put **100** as the denominator.

$\frac{23}{50} \xrightarrow{\times 2} \frac{46}{100} = 46\%$

Make an **equivalent fraction** with 100 as the denominator. The **numerator** is the percentage.

$\frac{6}{20} \xrightarrow{\times 5} \frac{30}{100} = 30\%$ are white

30% + 45% = 75% are white or black.
So **100**% − **75**% = **25**% are brown.

Percentages and Decimals

To convert a percentage to a decimal, **divide** by 100.
$37\% = 37 \div 100 = \mathbf{0.37}$

To convert a decimal to a percentage, **multiply** by 100.
$0.58 = 0.58 \times 100\% = \mathbf{58\%}$

Move the digits 2 places to the **right** to divide and 2 places to the **left** to multiply.

Fractions and Decimals

Make an **equivalent fraction** with 10, 100 or 1000 as the **denominator**.

Then read off the number of **tenths**, **hundredths** or **thousandths**.

$\frac{8}{25} \xrightarrow{\times 4} \frac{32}{100}$

This is **32 hundredths**, so $\frac{8}{25}$ is equivalent to **0.32**.

$\frac{12}{30} \xrightarrow{\div 3} \frac{4}{10}$

This is **4 tenths**, so $\frac{12}{30}$ is equivalent to **0.4**.

$3\frac{12}{30} = 3 + 0.4 = \mathbf{3.4}$

60 Answers

Answers

Pages 26-27 — Fractions, Decimals & Percentages Quiz

Key Words

1. **Mixed number**: A number that has a whole number part and a fraction part.
   Decimal place: Each number after the decimal point.
   Improper fraction: **A fraction where the numerator is bigger than the denominator.**
   (1 mark for each)

Key Diagrams

2. $\frac{1}{4}$ — Decimal: **0.25**
   Percentage: **25%**
   $\frac{3}{4}$ — Decimal: **0.75**
   Percentage: **75%**
   (1 mark for each)

Now Try These

3. 9 (1 mark)
4. Multiply it by 100. (1 mark)
5. Add the numerators. (1 mark)
6. Multiply or divide the numerator and the denominator by the same number. (1 mark)
7. Write all of the fractions as equivalent fractions using the common denominator. (1 mark)
8. 100 (1 mark)
9. 1. Multiply by the numerator.
   2. Divide by the denominator.
   (1 mark for each)

Measurement

Pages 28-29 — Converting Units

Converting Metric Units

Tables: 1 m = **100** cm
1 cm = **10** mm
1 kg = **1000** g
1 l = **1000** ml

Divide to go from a small unit to a bigger one.

1 kg = **1000** g

So divide by **1000**:

4260 ÷ **1000** = **4.26** kg

Put measurements in the **same** units before using them in calculations.

1 m = **100** cm

So **multiply** by **100**:

1.3 × **100** = **130** cm

130 − 22 = **108** cm tall

Converting Units of Time

1 week = **7** days,
so work out 128 ÷ **7**:

```
      1 8 r 2
  7 | 1 2 ⁵8
```

So it's **18** weeks and **2** days away.

1 hour = **60** minutes,
so 3 hours = 3 × **60** = **180** minutes

180 + 20 = **200** minutes

200 × 4 = **800** toys

Metric and Imperial Units

Type of unit: **Metric**
Type of unit: **Imperial**

Converting Imperial Units

masses

volumes

These are approximate conversions — they aren't exact. Write them using the sign ≈:

5 cm ≈ 2 inches

700 g ÷ **100** g = **7**,
so 700 g is **7** lots of **100** g.

That's about **7** lots of **4** ounces.

So 700 g ≈ **7** × **4** ounces
= **28** ounces

Pages 30-31 — Perimeter, Area and Volume

Finding Perimeters

To find the perimeter of a shape, **add** up the **lengths** of all of its sides.

If any side lengths are missing, use the other **lengths** to work them out.

The total width is 4 + **3** = **7** m.

So this side is **7** − **5** = **2** m.

The total length is 2 + **3** = **5** m.

So this side is **5** − 1 = **4** m.

Add up all the sides to find the perimeter: 4 + 2 + **3** + **3** + 5 + 1 + 2 + **4** = **24** m

Finding Areas

You can estimate the area of a shape on a grid by counting how many **squares** and half-**squares** it covers.

It covers **3** whole squares and **2** half-squares.

Area = **3** + $\frac{1}{2}$ + $\frac{1}{2}$ = **4** cm²

Answers

For more irregular shapes, count how many squares are more than **half** covered.

The area of this shape is about **5 cm²**.

Area is usually measured in '**square**' units:

cm² is **square** centimetres.

m² is **square metres**.

Areas of Squares and Rectangles

To find the area of a square or rectangle, **multiply** the length by the width.

So the area is **8 × 6 = 48 cm²**.

Area = **length** × width,
so 120 = **12** × width
120 ÷ **12** = **10**,
so the width is **10 m**.

Finding Volumes

Volume: the amount of **space** a 3D object takes up.

Volume is measured in '**cubic**' units:

cm³ is **cubic** centimetres.

m³ **cubic metres**.

There are 2 layers of **9** cubes each, so there are **9** × 2 = **18** cubes.

So the volume is **18 cm³**.

Capacity: the amount something can hold when it's **full**.

Pages 32-33 — Measurement Quiz

Key Words

1. **Metric unit**: A type of unit that includes kilograms, millimetres and litres.
   Imperial unit: A type of unit that includes pounds, miles and pints.
   Volume: **The amount of space a 3D object takes up.**
   Capacity: The amount something can hold when it's full.
   (1 mark for each)

Now Try These

2. False (1 mark)
3. Square centimetres (1 mark)
4. Add up the lengths of all of the shape's sides. (1 mark)
5. Multiply the number of hours by 60 (1 mark)
6. Multiply the length by the width. (1 mark)
7. ≈ (1 mark)
8. 5 cm² (1 mark)
9. a) 150 cm = **1.5** m
   b) 3.27 litres = **3270** ml
   (1 mark for each)

Geometry

Pages 34-35 — Angles

Angle Basics

Angles are measured in **degrees** (°).

90°
Right angle

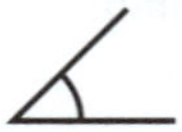

45° (half a **right** angle)

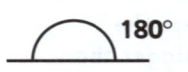

180°    270°

The angle is bigger than a **right** angle but smaller than one and a **half** right angles. So **110°** is a good estimate. (anything between **100°** and **120°** would be a sensible estimate)

Measuring and Drawing Angles

1 Put the bottom line of your **protractor** along one of the lines of the angle.

3 The angle is **34°**.

1 Draw a line and line up the **protractor** with it.

2 Read around the scale from **0** and mark where 52° is.

3 Join the end of the line to the mark. **Label** the angle.

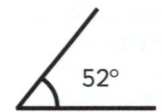

52°

Answers

Types of Angle

Acute angles are **less** than 90°.

Obtuse angles are **bigger** than 90° but **less** than 180°.

Reflex angles are bigger than 180°.

Angle Rules

1. Angles around a point add up to **360°**.
   a + b + c = **360°**
2. Angles on a **straight line** add up to **180°**.
   x + y + z = **180°**
3. Angles at a quarter turn add up to **90°**.
   p + q = **90°**

Pages 36-37 — Shapes

Regular and Irregular Polygons

A polygon is a 2D shape with straight **sides**.

Regular polygon: all sides are the same **length** and all angles are the same **size**.

This shape has **6** equal sides and **6** equal angles, so it is a **regular hexagon**.

Irregular polygon: does not have all **sides** the same length and all **angles** the same size.

This shape has **5** sides, but they are not all the same **length**, so it is an **irregular pentagon**.

Properties of Rectangles

1. **Opposite** sides of a rectangle are the same length.
2. All the angles in a rectangle are **right** angles.

Opposite sides are **equal**, so g = **7** cm

All angles are **right** angles, so h = **90°**

3D Shapes and Nets

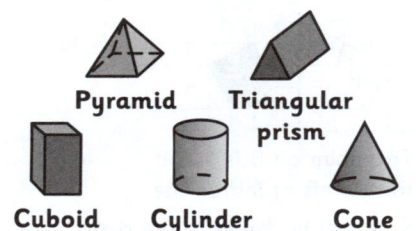

Pyramid, Triangular prism, Cuboid, Cylinder, Cone

A net is a **2D** shape that you can **fold** to make a **3D** shape. Each shape in the net is a **face** of the 3D shape.

Cube: E.g.

Triangular prism: E.g.

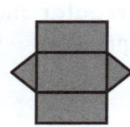

Plans and Elevations

Plan: how a shape looks from directly **above**.

Elevation: how a shape looks from one **side**.

Elevations can be different depending on whether you're looking at the shape from the **front** or the **side**.

Cuboid: Plan:

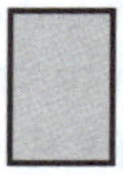

Square-based pyramid: Elevation:

Cylinder: Plan:

An arrow can be used to show the direction of the **elevation**.

Triangular prism:
Plan: Elevation:

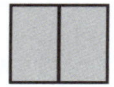

Pages 38-39 — Coordinates & Transformations

Coordinates

Coordinates give the **position** of a point on a grid. Read the **x**-coordinate first, then the **y**-coordinate.

The coordinates of the mug are (**8**, **3**).

Answers

Transformations

Transformation: a way of changing the **position** of a shape.

Translations

The shape doesn't change when it is reflected or **translated**.

Translations

Translation: when a shape slides from one position to another. Its **size** and **shape** don't change, and it doesn't rotate or flip over.

1. Pick a vertex. Move the correct number of squares, then mark a **cross**.
2. Repeat for each **vertex**.
3. Join up the **crosses**.

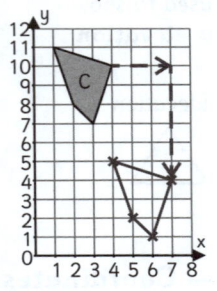

Reflections

Reflection: when a shape flips over a **mirror** line.
Its **size** and shape don't change, and it doesn't **rotate**.

A point and its **reflection** are always the same distance from the **mirror** line.

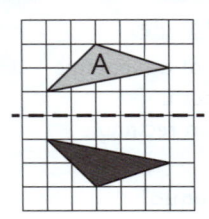

This point on A is **2** units **above** the mirror line.

So the reflected point will be **2** units **below** the mirror line.

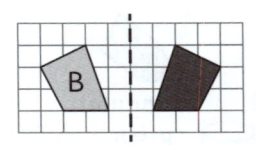

This point on B is **1** unit to the **left** of mirror line.

So it will be **1** unit to the **right** in the reflection.

Symmetry

Line of Symmetry: a **mirror line** drawn through a shape so that the shape is the **same** on both sides of the line.

All **regular** polygons (and some **irregular** ones) have lines of symmetry.

Pages 40-41 — Geometry Quiz

Key Words

1. **Line of symmetry**: A mirror line drawn through a shape so that the shape is the same on both sides of the line.
   Transformation: **A way of changing the position of a shape.**
   Elevation: **How a shape looks from one side.**
   Polygon: A 2D shape with straight sides.
   (1 mark for each)

Now Try These

2. Degrees (°) (1 mark)
3. 4 cm (1 mark)
4. 360° (1 mark)
5. Acute (1 mark)
6. Put the bottom line of your protractor along one of the lines of the angle. (1 mark)
7.

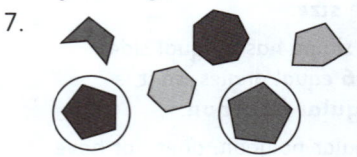

   (1 mark for both circled)
8. 3 units to the left of the mirror line (1 mark)
9. a) Cuboid (1 mark)
   b) Rectangle (1 mark)
10. W (1 mark)

Answers

Statistics

Pages 42-43 — Line Graphs

Reading Off Line Graphs

Line Graphs: show how something **changes**.

Find the information you're given on one **axis**.

Move across or down to the other **axis** and read off the value.

280 tickets were sold on day 2.

340 tickets were sold on day **3**.

Line Graph Problems

To find totals, read off the values and **add** them together.

30 apples were sold.

45 apples were sold.

So **30** + **45** = **75** apples were sold in total on Thursday and Friday.

To find differences, read off the values and **subtract** them.

Read up from the '**Time**' axis:

At 11 am, there were **8** children.

At 3 pm, there were **12** children.

12 − **8** = **4** more children were at the park at 3 pm.

Comparing Line Graphs

After 2 minutes, Maya had run **0.5** km and Clare had run **0.25** km.

To run 1.5 km, it took Maya **6** minutes and Clare **10** minutes.

The **key** tells you what each line represents.

Pages 44-45 — Tables

Reading Off Tables

Read off information by finding the correct **row** and **column**.

25 cups of coffee were sold on Saturday.

10 + **16** = **26** cups of tea were sold in total.

16 + **14** + 10 = **40** hot drinks were sold on Sunday.

Completing Tables

8 people chose rabbit,
so **8** + **2** = **10** people chose dog.

12 people chose cat,
so **12** ÷ **2** = **6** people chose hamster.

40 − 12 − **10** − 8 − **6**
 = **4** people chose fish.

Reading Timetables

Each **column** shows the times for one bus.

The 09:50 bus from the Town Centre gets to Park Avenue at **10:02**.

+ **7**

+ **8**

The journey from the Town Centre to the Sports Centre takes 5 + **7** + **8** = **20** minutes.

Timetable Problems

Find the **row** for Rodentonia and read across.

2:50 pm is the same as **14:50**.
The last time before **14:50** is **14:04**.

Read up the **column** to Mouseley. Jack should catch the **13:20** train.

Pages 46-47 — Statistics Quiz

Key Words

1. Line graph: **A graph that shows how something changes.**
   Table: A way of showing data using rows and columns.
   Timetable: A chart that shows when things are happening.
   (1 mark for each)

Now Try These

2. Subtract the number of pupils with brown, blonde and black hair from the total number of pupils in the class. (1 mark)

3. Read off the values and subtract them. (1 mark)

4. She should read across the row to find the last time before 11:20. (1 mark)

5. a) Day 3 (1 mark)
   b) 40 + **30** = **70** push ups
   (1 mark)

Answers   65

Answers

Pages 48-53 — End of Year Quiz

Key Words

1. **Negative numbers**: Numbers that are less than zero.
   Volume: The amount of space a 3D object takes up.
   Regular polygon: **A polygon where all sides are the same length and all angles are the same size.**
   Line graph: A type of graph that shows how something changes.
   Prime number: A number that has exactly two factors: 1 and itself.
   Square number: **The number you get when you multiply a number by itself.**
   Acute angle: **An angle smaller than 90°.**
   Common factor: A number that is a factor of two (or more) numbers.
   (1 mark for each)

2. Plan: **How a shape looks from directly above.**
   Elevation: **How a shape looks from one side.**
   Net: **A 2D shape that you can fold to make a 3D shape.**
   (1 mark for each)

3. **Improper fraction**: A fraction where the numerator is bigger than the denominator.
   Mixed number: A number that has a whole number part and a fraction part.
   Equivalent fraction: A fraction that looks different to another fraction, but is equal to it.
   (2 marks for all correct, otherwise 1 mark for one correct)

4. Transformation: A way of changing the **position** of a shape.
   Translation: When a shape slides from one position to another.
   Reflection: When a shape flips over a **mirror** line.
   (1 mark for each)

Now Try These

5. **12 48 24 (32) 18** (1 mark)
6. Irregular (1 mark)
7. 90° (1 mark)
8. 3 (1 mark)
9. Compare the numerators (1 mark)
10. 270° (1 mark)
11. 10 (1 mark)
12. 100% − 46% = 54% (1 mark)
13. 100 (1 mark)
14. False (1 mark)
15. Subtract the smaller numeral from the bigger one (1 mark)
16. Two places to the right (1 mark)
17. a) $1\frac{4}{9}$ b) $3\frac{3}{4}$
    (1 mark for each)
18. **2** or **5** (1 mark for both)
19. There are 2 layers of 8 cubes, so 2 × 8 = 16 cubes in total. So the volume is 16 cm³. (1 mark)
20. Ones (1 mark)
21. a) 12 + 7 = 19 (1 mark)
    b) 7 + 4 + 7 = 18 (1 mark)
22. Find equivalent fractions that have a common denominator. (1 mark)
23. Do 40 × 7 and 1 × 7, then subtract. (1 mark)
24. a) 5 − 3 = 2 cm (1 mark)
    b) 2 + 1 + 3 + 3 + 5 + 2 = 16 cm (1 mark)
25. a) 1 kg ≈ 2 pounds, so 5 kg ≈ 5 × 2 = 10 pounds (1 mark)
    b) 2 pounds ≈ 1 kg, so 20 pounds ≈ 20 ÷ 2 = 10 kg (1 mark)
26. a) 11 (1 mark)
    b) She saw 14 sparrows and 7 blackbirds, so she saw 14 − 7 = 7 more sparrows. (1 mark)
27. Square-based pyramid (1 mark)
28. C (1 mark)
29. a) 26 minutes (1 mark)
    b) 15:48 (1 mark)